Starched
CAPS
collars
AND CUffS

JAN O'LEARY

Starched

Caps

Collars

and Cuffs

MEMOIRS

Cirencester

Published by Memoirs

MEMOIRS
PUBLISHING

Memoirs Books

25 Market Place, Cirencester, Gloucestershire, GL7 2NX
info@memoirsbooks.co.uk www.memoirspublishing.com

ISBN 978-1-909020-22-1

Printed in England

Starched
CAPS
collars
AND CUFFS

Contents

Introduction
Dedication and acknowledgments

Introduction

I am a typical character born under the sign of Gemini, a dual personality always able to multi-function. My strengths include a loving interest in people, a deep nurturing instinct and effective communication skills. These were all fulfilled during my active nursing life as a wife, a mother of one son and four daughters and as a personnel manager in industry.

In retirement I dabbled in a small village shop for two years, which proved a very expensive hobby, followed by four years as a voluntary case worker for SSAFFA.

I left school at sixteen and went into nursing. For the next eight years I worked in England and Hong Kong, followed by twelve years as an Army officer's lady, when I spent most of the time pregnant. This was followed by a period of active salaried employment until I retired in 1991. Retirement was anything but relaxing when family trauma dictated how it would be spent.

Throughout this long and full life I have needed to wear many hats, some of which have fitted better than others. Those of my early years were replaced by a net on a factory floor, Jackie Kennedy pillboxes and high-fashion cartwheels, but the ones I got most satisfaction from wearing were the white starched ones.

My interest in the progress and regress of what was a nursing profession has remained. I have sadly witnessed its decline since the late 1980s, when the previous excellent nurse training system was unwisely changed.

Dedication and acknowledgments

To my husband and children, who never minded which hat I was wearing but supported me while I was wearing all of them. I salute all the State Registered Nurses who did their nurse training prior to Project 2000 and who were dedicated to a once-proud profession which gave a caring service for the benefit of their patients. With appreciation to the doctors at Ixworth Surgery, who have restored my faith in the medical profession, and especially Dr John Cannon, who set such high standards. Also to Diana, who encouraged me to write about being passed my 'sell by date'.

With special thanks to Chris Newton, Editor who has updated and tweaked my prose and also to Tony Tingle for publishing my wish to 'justify my existence'.

For Catherine

With my loving thank yours
for your care and
kindness
Jan
Sept 2012

Chapter One

IN AT THE DEEP END

'Now girls, I wish to know what your future plans are!'

It was the beginning of the 1950s. Miss Willoughby, a tall elegant lady, stood in front of the class of girls and asked us in turn what we wanted to do when we left the grammar school.

I was sixteen, and all I had ever wanted to do was become a nurse. The other students who had been asked the question all appeared to have a desire to do something glamorous, or at least highly professional, such as medicine and law. So when the headmistress asked me what my future plans were, I answered that I wanted to be a dress designer.

This wise lady was not taken in by my bravado and questioned me about my marks for art. They were not especially promising, so I quickly commented that designing was just a fantasy and realistically I had set my heart on nursing.

The look of relief on her face was evident. She immediately suggested that I could leave school and start nursing without staying on to take a higher school certificate. This was music to my ears, as I had no desire to continue a twelve-hour day. The innocence of youth precluded me from knowing how many hours nurses worked each day.

To get to school from the small Yorkshire village near to which my family lived, I had to catch a steam train from a small station at 7.30 am. It stopped at every platform en route to York (this was long before Dr Beeching axed all the branch lines). The return journey in the evening was twelve hours later, so I tried to do my homework before journey's end.

There was a one-mile walk from and to both stations, which was enjoyable during the summer months but grim when snow lay deep and the wind was icy. After a long winter it was always a relief to see the crowds of daffodils covering the castle wall embankment outside the city railway station and to know that spring had arrived.

It was against my father's wishes that I was embarking on a nursing career, as it meant living away from home. His attitude made me more determined than ever to escape the strict confines of family life. I was fortunate in having a head teacher who cared about her students leaving school and achieving their ambitions, and she arranged an interview with the matron of an orthopaedic hospital on the Yorkshire moors, the Adela Shaw Hospital in Kirbymoorside.

Orthopaedic nursing training could be started at sixteen years of age, and took two years. This fitted in well, as I could not start my general training until I was eighteen. Before then I had to be accepted. At the beginning of the summer holidays I caught a local bus and attended the interview in the hospital, which was fifteen miles from my home.

On arrival at the hospital I was shown into an office, which was a very stark, dreary room furnished with a desk and two chairs. Soon afterwards a very stern figure came in, wearing a navy blue dress with long sleeves, stiffly starched collar, cuffs and a large white cap; there was not a wisp of hair revealed under this edifice, a silver badge and belt buckle being the only adornments. She introduced herself as Matron and then handed me an examination paper, telling me that I should complete it within forty minutes.

I was then left alone. Reading the questions, I was very relieved to find that they appeared easier than I expected and were mostly general knowledge, with a few about my own personal interests, such as hobbies and my reading likes and dislikes. Finally I had to say why I wanted to be a nurse. Wondering if I should try to impress by saying it was because it was a vocation or if I should say that I really wanted to be a doctor but had decided to care rather than cure, I finally wrote that it was because I liked the uniform. It seemed to me that it was time to abandon my navy blue gymslip, white shirt, striped tie and girdle for something more attractive.

When I was once more confronted by the imposing lady responsible for employing new nurses, I was pleasantly surprised to hear her ask me, 'When can you commence employment?' Perhaps she was not really interested in the answers I had given on the paper. Perhaps she was simply short of staff and needed an extra pair of hands.

At that time a German pen-friend was staying at my home. We had been encouraged to communicate with girls of our own ages who lived in Germany, supposedly to improve our knowledge of the language, or perhaps it was to try and build bridges, as it was only seven years since the end of the war. Her own English was excellent and she was determined to practise it at every opportunity. That suited me, because I had no desire to practice that guttural language. However I could not wait to start work in the hospital, so I replied to Matron's query by telling her I could start the following day.

When I arrived home and broke the news to my parents, I threw our home into a frenzy of activity. I had been given a list of requisites. I needed three of each of the items of clothing I was expected to provide, along with a pair of black lace-up shoes and black stockings. The village shop did not stock these, so once my mother gave up trying to persuade me to contact Matron Lilley and tell her I needed to postpone the start date, there was a hurried visit to York.

Having collected all the kit, which was packed into a battered cardboard suitcase, a relic of the war years, I set forth the next day by village bus, leaving mother to improve her non-existent German on her own.

Chapter Two

BEDPANS & BLACK STOCKINGS

The Adela Shaw Hospital was approached from the main road through tall double wrought-iron gates and a long drive, and it comprised a series of wooden huts raised off the ground. During the Second World War it had been a military hospital. There were four wards, an administration block, a long connecting corridor and a main kitchen. In the grounds were an isolation ward, a workshop and a nurses' home. There were also separate detached houses for Matron, two doctors and the nurses on night duty.

On arrival I was shown into my room in the nurses' home by a portly motherly figure with the position of Home Sister, called Sister Sinclair. The home was a long hutted building which contained single rooms, bathrooms and two large sitting rooms, one for the students and one for the qualified staff. My room was spacious, well furnished and spotlessly clean, with a highly-polished wooden floor, divan bed, wardrobe and desk-cum-dressing table, a small bedside locker and a rug. It was the first time I had had a room to call my own, having always had to share with a sibling. It was worth leaving home to have a room to myself.

On the bed was a pile of neatly-folded uniforms: three sets of blue cotton drill dresses, white starched aprons, collars and caps. A laundry bag was there for future dirty linen. I unpacked my suitcase, carefully hanging up the clothes and uniforms on wire hangers in the wardrobe before venturing into the sitting room, where I was told I could find a cup of tea. Several student nurses were in there having their mid-morning break. It lasted only fifteen minutes, so they were obviously anxious to drink as much as possible in a short time and polish off the plate of biscuits.

I was given a cursory look up and down and a few welcoming smiles, and asked my surname. For the next two years I was known only as Tedstill, both on and off duty. The room suddenly became empty and I was again left to my own devices.

I was not sure if I should put on my uniform and report to the main office. Deciding to play safe rather than give the wrong impression, I thought that I would show willing, so I struggled into the very stiff dress, fumbled with the Peter Pan starched collar, which had to be attached with collar studs, and endeavoured to fold the cap so that it resembled those worn by the girls I had seen sipping their cups of tea. Next on were the black stockings, to be held up by a suspender belt, and then the shoes. I placed a new fountain pen and scissors in a breast pocket, pinned my fob watch on to it, and finally put on the apron, the bib of which had to be pinned to the dress with two safety pins.

Looking into the mirror I was amazed to find that I actually looked like a nurse. Perhaps I really had chosen the right career.

Then I had to decide what to do next. I was saved from making a decision by a knock on the door. I was confronted by another new student who had found out that we were to go across the garden to another hutted building which housed the classrooms.

She took one look at my cap and laughed out loud. She suggested I should take it off, and said she would refold it in the correct manner. She had a sister who had started at the same hospital two years earlier, so Valerie King was very knowledgeable about what and what not to do, and was a very useful ally.

On entering the classroom we were introduced to Sister Clark, the tutor, and four other new girls who had arrived to start their orthopaedic training over the previous few days. They looked like a friendly bunch and were all sixteen years old.

On each of their desks was an object which I presumed was a bone. I had never previously seen any kind of bone other than a mutton bone after the Sunday lunch had been eaten, but it was fairly clear that these were human. I guessed that the longest was a thigh bone. The skull and vertebrae were easily identified. I was not sure about the other long bones, but guessed that I was about to find out.

We spent the next few weeks not only finding out which bones were which but learning the names of all the knobbly protrusions, joints, muscles and ligament attachments. We had to draw them all from memory, naming each part and producing immaculate diagrams as if they were going to be published in Gray's Anatomy.

The other practical teaching sessions were spent bandaging. We learned how to use all the various kinds for appropriate purposes, applying them in a precise way with the pattern depending on whether they were for a limb, body or head. We would practise on each other, and at the end of a session we would all be bandaged from head to toe until we looked like Egyptian mummies.

We learned how to make beds with and without an occupant, each time perfecting the hospital corners and achieving the correct top sheet width turned over the red-top blanket and the placing of pillows with the openings away from the main entrance to the ward. Trolleys had to be laid according to their purpose. We had to learn how to bed-bath patients, again using each other, with the victims wearing bathing costumes. We injected oranges with sterile water, resorting to sandbags if all the oranges had been eaten. We learned how to fill hot-water bottles correctly so that the near-boiling water would not spit back at us.

There were also lectures on hygiene, etiquette and ethics, all accompanied by notes neatly written in notebooks and handed in for correction. This was before we were then taught physiology.

Referring back to my ancient lecture notes, I read that emphasis was placed on hospital etiquette. This was to reflect the customs practised in the hospital, which were founded on good manners and respect for seniority. Certain rules had been laid out by the hospital authorities. As with all communities, a certain amount of discipline had to be maintained for the comfort and wellbeing of all concerned.

I went on to read the rules regarding the nurses' professional conduct towards the patients. I only wish today's nurses could have these instilled into them during their training. We were taught the Hippocratic Oath and the rules relating to our behaviour towards our superiors. When on duty, the matron and administration staff were only to be addressed in connection with matters of duty.

Doctors had to be addressed as Sir, surgeons as Mr and physicians as Doctor. I wondered why – I had imagined they were all just doctors. We were told that it was common politeness to open doors and make way for people in a superior position, and always to stand when Matron or a doctor came in. I never had to practise this, because I was never allowed to sit down when on duty anyway. I certainly never met them when I was off duty.

Domestic staff, who included the ward maids, had to be treated with courtesy but never familiarity. They were often old enough to be our mothers or even our grandmothers. It soon became clear that they should be cherished, as they could be relied on to guide and protect one's interests provided you did not make a muddle in their kitchen or mark their polished ward floors.

I am still in the habit of arriving at least two minutes early for any appointment, which goes back to those initial rules. It was many years before I could relax in the presence of any superior, on or off duty, and it took a lot of self-discipline not to call a doctor boyfriend 'sir'.

Reading through the old nursing notes, I have found a reference to making beds by different methods according to the patients' medical condition, which then goes on to refer to 'different positions in bed', if my memory is correct. I do not remember a titter among the sixteen-year-olds when this heading was dictated by the tutor. No doubt today's students would react differently. In the 1950s though, at that tender age, we were all fairly naive.

Initial forays on to the wards were daunting. Stepping through the main ward door for the first time was nerve-racking when thirty plus pairs of eyes turned to peer at you, mostly from above bed covers. My first ward's occupants were boys and girls aged three to seven years old, the youngest in iron cots and the older children in small beds. The long ward was the Florence Nightingale type, with a row of beds and cots on either side, and there was a glass-fronted office halfway down with a kitchen next to it. The sluices and bathrooms were at each end of the ward. The wards were like the nurses' home, all wooden huts, but they also had long verandahs down one of the long sides which had folding shutter doors so that they could be opened.

Many of the children came from deprived areas of large towns or cities and were suffering from diseases caused by poverty, especially from tuberculosis of various joints. A common source of this disease was unpasteurised milk. It was considered beneficial for their limbs to be immobilised with splints and for these children to be fed a simple but healthy diet and exposed to fresh air by pushing their cots and beds out on to the verandahs throughout the year. I can still remember small faces with red noses to match their blankets, woolly hats, scarves and gloves providing some defence against the snowflakes settling on and around them.

These children remained in hospital for several years, and few saw their parents during this time. Shortage of money often prevented relations from visiting; few people owned cars and bus travel was not possible from such distances. The nurses undertook more than nursing duties, and tried to provide social activities for these youngsters, so we learned how to nurture as well as nurse and provide various forms of recreation. We took the children on picnics to the seaside, to pick bilberries on the moors and anywhere an ambulance and coach could go. Once at our destination we would use wheelchairs or stretchers where necessary.

At that time many children had disabilities associated with polio and were admitted for the application of splints to support limbs. One small boy had lost the use of both his arms and became very adept at using his toes for holding a spoon or pencil.

There was one surgeon who himself had been a polio victim and had a distinct limp. He was the only surgeon I ever met who insisted on being called Dr and not Mr, and he was affectionately known as Pop, not in a paternal way but because of his profuse use of plaster of Paris, POP.

To gain an orthopaedic nursing certificate took two years' training, the first year being identical to that given in a general hospital. We had examinations at the end of each year, both written and practical. The second year was concentrated on more advanced treatments of dressings, injections, blood transfusions and how to manage the ward. This was particularly important when we were left alone to run a ward on night duty. This duty came round twice each year, the first time just six months after joining.

My first three months of night duty was on a ward for boys aged seven to seventeen years, so the eldest was actually a few months older than I was. He was a law unto himself. He was mobile following extensive surgery for a TB hip joint; this had been surgically made permanently stiff and he wore a leather leg spica for support.

He was always disappearing, especially at bedtime. On my first night on duty I found him hiding under a pile of blankets on the top shelf of a spacious walk-in airing cupboard. I had searched everywhere else until one of the younger boys took pity on me and told me where to look. Until then I had begun to imagine being dismissed for losing a patient.

The twelve-hour night shifts were reasonably quiet. After lights were out, green shades were put round the wall lights near the post-operative cases. Stone hot-water bottles had been refilled to dry out plaster of Paris casts, a pencil marking the outline of any haemorrhage which had come through the plaster so that we could tell if there was any further bleeding.

Having ensured that the boys had all settled down to sleep I had to start on a pile of mending and darning. I knew the skill learned at Brownies would be useful one day, but I had hoped it would be as a wife and mother, not as a lonely student nurse sitting in a cold ward sister's office with a curtain firmly across the window.

The curtain did not stop the local village boys from scratching on the window to try to attract the attention of the nurse on duty. I had been warned that this would happen and that under no circumstances were they to be encouraged.

The only perk of these lonely hours was my discovery of a hoard of sweets. Two large fitted cupboards covered two sides of the office and were connected at the corner. The side which housed the sweet rations was padlocked, but by carefully squeezing through the opposite, unlocked cupboard I could reach the sweet tin. I thought if I only removed one goodie at a time Sister would not notice. I suppose that before I meet my maker I should confess this misdemeanour!

There was so much work to do at waking-up time that instead of waiting for six am, the earliest time we were supposed to awaken the patients, I was starting at least an hour earlier, taking a bowl of warm water, a face cloth and a towel around to each of the bed-bound children, washing their hands and faces, reapplying their splints and telling them to go back to sleep. The day sister soon realised what was happening when Sister Fox felt the facecloths and towels and found they were all bone dry. I had to appear in front of Matron to explain why I had felt it necessary to cut corners. I was not alone, as another nurse on a ward which had children from three to seven years had been caught doing a similar thing.

Together Mary Chadney, the other nurse, and I had enough courage to face this stern lady and tell her that it was impossible to wash all the children separately, dress those who were mobile, apply bandages and splints, take temperatures, pulses and respirations and make over thirty beds, all in one and a half hours, working on our own.

In her wisdom, she agreed that the day staff expectations were unrealistic. From the very next day she introduced a new system. One of the day duty students would work a shift from 6 am to 3 pm and come on to the ward to help the night nurse perform all the duties. This was a shift which I preferred when it came to my turn. It was bliss finishing mid afternoon for a whole week, and on fine days I could get on my bike and cycle all round the moors.

This exercise only lasted until I acquired a boyfriend with a powerful motor bike. I had met him at a Saturday evening village dance. I rode pillion, without a helmet. This was before safety helmets were made compulsory, and also before I had to nurse the shattered victims of motor-cycle accidents with horrendous head injuries. After that I never rode anything more powerful than a Lambretta.

During the first year we were given an insight into physiology, had experience on the girls' ward and observed tonsillectomies in the operating theatre which were performed on children from the local area. It wasn't quite done on the kitchen table but I can still smell that dreadful ether, which was dripped on to the face masks of the patients to render them unconscious, and the after-effects of the nausea. We then had a practical and written examination, at the time not realising that it would be a dress rehearsal for the one we would be taking at the end of our first year in general nurse training.

The second year followed a similar pattern to the first, but with more in-depth application and increased responsibilities. I was very pleased that the bedpan rounds were now undertaken by the new intake of nurses and the heavy wooden bed side lockers which had to be scrubbed every Monday could also be delegated.

When my own year group started their training there was a history of bullying by the second-year students, and one of my colleagues was treated so badly that she had a nervous breakdown. This tradition came to a swift end when we were in the senior position and refused to continue this intimidating and cruel practice.

To take our final practical examination we had to travel to South Yorkshire, to Pinderfields Hospital near Wakefield. This was a hospital which specialised in spinal injuries, many of the injuries having been sustained in the coal mines.

I had one practical session with two examiners who handed me a spinal column and asked me to identify the different sections, naming all the various protrusions, muscles and ligaments, the adjoining joints and the diseases and injuries which could affect it. Little did I know then that in years to come I would become familiar with every ache and pain which could result in spinal injury, and I still wonder why we ever started to walk up right.

The second session was applying splints, bandages and weights to a young man's legs and putting them into traction. This entailed cutting the Holland plaster, which resembled a fly paper and was equally sticky, especially after it was placed on to the lid of a stainless steel steriliser containing boiling water. The secret was not to heat it up too much after cutting it to the right leg lengths, put it on before it lost its stickiness and then apply the bandages, using a very neat pattern with each turn exactly the same width as the previous ones.

The cord with the weights at the end had to be attached to its end. I cannot remember which knot was used but it was probably a reef, as any slippage would not have helped the fractured limb. The man was very good-looking and he had lost or let slip his modesty triangle, which resembled a bikini bottom with ties at the sides. This did not help my concentration!

This was followed by laying up a trolley for the administration of an intravenous blood transfusion. On reflection I am sure I forgot the bag of blood for the infusion, even after checking the patient's blood group.

As I waited anxiously for the results of the examination, ward work continued. At the tender age of eighteen I was frequently left in charge of the boys' ward, where I felt very superior to the new students. It was only after being summoned to Matron's office that I realised it was not such a privilege to be in this exalted position, because she accused me of not keeping a close eye on the new recruits - not on duty but after lights out in the nurses' home. The night sister had seen them climbing through their bedroom windows after midnight. They obviously had more courage than my year group.

Some of the friends I made at the Adela Shaw Hospital have remained throughout my life. Valerie and I are still in touch, and in later years when one of my daughters had an operation for the removal of a brain tumour in a neurosurgical hospital near where she lived, my husband and I were made very welcome guests there.

Earning only four pounds nine shillings a month and always hard up, we pooled clothes and jewellery if one of us was going out. The main social event was a Saturday evening dance in one of the local village halls. There we jived and ballroom-danced to the music of the 1950s. Johnnie Rae was very popular for his ballads, Chris Barber for traditional jazz and then later in the decade Bill Haley played rock and roll. In my early teens my taste in music changed from the strings of Mantovani to the latest pop.

The two years' training came to an end when we obtained our orthopaedic certificates, which were beautifully written on a parchment scroll and signed by Lord Nuffield. We then had to decide where to do our general nursing training. Several of my colleagues, apart from one who came with me, chose to remain in Yorkshire, going either to Leeds or York. Because I never took the easy route I travelled all the way to Essex, packing my belongings in two battered suitcases but leaving a cardboard box of notebooks and ornaments with an acquaintance in the village. I never did go back to retrieve them and wonder how long they remained in that box. Perhaps they still lie covered in a film of dust and cobwebs in an attic, to be found by a future generation. They may even wonder why there are so many illustrations of the human body.

August 1952 - April 1955
Adela Shaw Orthopaedic Hospital, North Yorkshire

April 1955 - April 1959
Chelmsford and Essex Hospital

Staff nurse with
convalescent patients

Main door, Matron's office on right

Chapter Three

NURSING SCHOOL

I didn't even have to attend an interview to get a place at the Chelmsford and Essex School of Nursing. One matron accepted a recommendation from another, and the extra bonus of my orthopaedic nursing qualification sealed it.

My first view of the Chelmsford and Essex Hospital came as I alighted from the double-decker bus I had caught from the railway station. From the roadside it appeared a very stark, grey building with a Victorian exterior softened by two large bay windows on either side of a huge wooden door. On trembling legs I crossed the wide asphalt frontage, which seemed a vast expanse of ground. No doubt these days it is covered in cars.

I entered the building and saw immediately opposite me over a tiled hall a glass-fronted porters' desk. The head porter peered at me over his specs and summoned me to approach. He told me to leave my suitcases in his domain and then to knock on the matron's door. I had passed this just after entering through the main door. Perhaps Matron Jones had seen me through her bay window and wondered at my hesitation.

I was reassured when this diminutive lady beckoned me to sit opposite her, welcomed me to the C&E and asked me if I had had a comfortable journey. She told me I would be taken to my room by the home sister, appropriately named Sister Holmes, whom the porter would have informed of my arrival. Such efficiency impressed and enthralled me.

My new abode was a pleasant room, furnished starkly but adequately. It overlooked the front, so for the first time I would hear traffic through my window. Being brought up in the country, the only nocturnal noises I had heard previously were the hooting of owls, or the crowing of cockerels as dawn approached.

My new uniform was laid on the bed, a bundle of grey and white stripe tied up with a length of cotton fabric. The home sister told me where I could meet the other new students and where to find the dining room for tea, and gave me the programme for the following day's induction in the nursing training school.

The single-storey dining room overlooked the Essex County Cricket Club field, but do not imagine we ever managed to watch even a few minutes of a match through its windows. When we were in there we were like horses with their heads in their nosebags, hoping that we might be fortunate enough to grab second helpings.

There was a very definite pecking order in the dining hall, everyone segregated according to their seniority. It was easy for me to discern who the newest students were by their anxious faces, mufti clothes and the position of the long table where they were seated. With trepidation I ventured forth, gave them my surname and asked if I could join them. My previous experience made the step up to a large hospital an easy transition. I could at least recognise the sisters by their navy blue dresses and large starched caps, and I had the sense not to go and sit at their table.

On first approaching the dining room I could also see several white-coated figures at the far end, in an area divided from the nurses' section by a wooden partition. Obviously it was the doctors' area with the most advantageous view of the cricket field, and probably a more appetizing menu than was available to us mortals.

My first year in general training was just like the last year, and was a repetition of what I had already accomplished. My friend from Yorkshire and I were well ahead of our new colleagues, who had not been on a ward before starting their general training.

Our proficiency meant we were very readily accepted on our first wards, but before that we had to spend three months in the nursing school, where we had lectures from the senior tutor, Miss Brett an ex-army nursing major, and practical tuition from a tutor. Mrs Bunch was a motherly figure, with white curly hair and a rounded shape, a sweet smile and gentle demeanour. This was in stark contrast to the very military bearing of the lady who lectured us from the front of the classroom.

Our blue cotton dresses were exchanged for grey and white striped ones, Sister Dora caps, black shoes and stockings. The hems of our dresses had to reach the floor when we knelt down, preventing a glimpse of our thighs when we bent over the beds. Our white cotton aprons were stiffly starched and the collars were so stiff that they rubbed our necks, often leaving marks which could be mistaken for love bites.

Once again we worked long hours on the wards, and in the evenings we all collapsed in the nurse's home sitting room, impatient to kick off our shoes and rest our aching and weary feet. The television with the small eight-inch screen was only rarely viewed, the black and white pictures holding little interest.

My first ward placement was on the female surgical ward on the first floor, a long Nightingale ward with a light, airy day room at the furthest end from the main door into the ward. Sister Hyman's office was immediately on the right as you entered, with two side wards next to it. The ward kitchen was the domain of a very 'in command' ward maid nearby.

The atmosphere here was always very pleasant, the tone being set by a very strict but fair sister in charge. The senior staff nurse Eastman was someone every student nurse wanted to emulate. She not only looked attractive but was adored by the patients, their male relatives and the medical staff.

Down the centre of the ward was a long cupboard unit with a continuous worktop on to which the numerous vases of flowers were placed at night. These were always plentiful, and my favourite treat was arranging them during visiting hours, if I could escape from the sluice.

The sluice was the coldest part of the ward. It held racks containing stainless steel bed pans, a washer into which used ones were placed, rows of urine testing equipment, sputum pots and specimen jars, and it became the domain, and sometimes the sanctuary, of every first-year nurse.

Bedpan rounds were routine, immediately after meals, when peeing or pooing was expected to order. The pans were first warmed up under running hot water, wiped, placed on a trolley concealed with a cloth, curtains drawn around the beds and a screen erected to conceal this ritual from anyone daring to enter the ward at this time.

I once made the mistake of not warming a pan for an elderly 'fractured hip' patient who had refused to sit on one at the allocated time but then insisted she was desperate just as I was going for my lunch. When I assisted her on to the pan, she made no signs that it was icy but dropped a hankie onto the floor under her bed, requesting that I retrieve it. As I was bending down she whipped out the bed pan from under her shrivelled back side and firmly struck me on the back of my head. I collapsed in a heap on the floor, looked up at her in astonishment and found that she was doubled up in laughter. Thank goodness she had yet to perform, so the empty pan did nothing but diminish my dignity. The old lady and I understood each other and I never took short cuts again.

After the bed pans the next trolley round was the 'backs'. Every bed patient had to have their pressure areas rubbed, first with soap and water, then with surgical spirits and finally powder. I think the actual rubbing did more good than the application of anything, as the circulation was stimulated with firm but gentle massage.

The only pressure sores I witnessed were on a young paraplegic man who had driven alone from Johannesburg across the Sahara to London, and had to be admitted to our private wards suffering from the after-effects of such a long endurance test.

Bed-making with and without an occupant was a team exercise with two nurses working in tandem, one on either side of the bed. The bed was first stripped by one of two methods. Every cover was folded into three, left over right, or in a Z fashion, and placed over two chairs at the foot of the bed. Having tightly straightened the bottom sheet the top covers were replaced in turn, with hospital corners precisely executed and the top sheet turned over to exactly the same width throughout the ward. If this procedure went to plan, each unoccupied bed took only three minutes to make, which was just as well with 32 to make, twice per day.

TPRs (temperature, pulse and respirations) were recorded every four hours, more frequently when a patient was being closely monitored. In the 1950s in my previous hospital, if a student broke a thermometer it had to be taken to Matron for a replacement, which cost the nurse ten shillings. Woe betide the nurse who dropped the tray and broke them all.

Each thermometer was put into a small glass jar which had a piece of cotton wool at the bottom and then it was topped up with an antiseptic mouthwash solution. These were carried from patient to patient on an enamel tray. It was fortunate that in Chelmsford progress had been made, and each bed had its own thermometer in a test tube fixed to the wall behind the bed head.

Blood pressures were monitored four hourly and a cuff was wound around the upper arm before being pumped up, then a stethoscope was used to listen for the beats as the mercury crept up the glass tube.

Everything was recorded on a chart in the patients' notes, which were on a clipboard at the foot of each bed. I once made the mistake of reading my own notes when as a patient I was hospitalised. The doctor had referred to me as 'This pale plump pleasant person', not taking into consideration the fact that I was seven months pregnant and anaemic at the time. I had managed to keep calm and not panic at being on the receiving rather than the giving end of care.

There were no central treatment wards for the renewal of dressings, so trolleys were also laid up for doing dressing rounds on the general ward, the advantage being that all the patient care was undertaken by the ward staff. This also included pre and post-operative care, there being no recovery or intensive care wards.

On routine operation days, a junior nurse accompanied the patient to the theatre and remained there to observe the procedure before returning with the patient to the ward. She would often feel very anxious while waiting by the bedside for the patient to come round from the anaesthetic.

During my second week on female surgical I was detailed to accompany a theatre case and followed the theatre porters, who were pushing the trolley with the patient dozing as the effects of the premedication injection took hold. Arriving in the anaesthetic room I was instructed to put on a long green gown which tied down the back, tie my hair up in a green cotton square, apply a face mask and wear white rubber boots. There was very little left to see apart from my eyes. In the meantime the anaesthetist, Doctor Pim Stiggelbout was beginning the administration of the intravenous needle into the patient's vein. The patient was told to count, but she got no further than five, when she was wheeled unconscious into the adjoining operating theatre. I expected there to be a reverent hush but there was a hubbub of activity, the surgeon cracking a joke with a nurse similarly gowned to myself. There was another gowned figure standing behind a trolley which contained rows of shiny instruments and a large bright light illuminated the table on to which the patient was lifted. The anaesthetist sat at the patient's head, next to a trolley containing various cylinders, presumably containing different gases - oxygen and nitrous oxygen was my guess.

A member of the theatre staff showed me where to stand so that I could see what was going on without being in anyone's way. Feeling surplus to requirements but interested, I tried to look invisible.

My charge and I returned to the ward immediately after the final sutures had been inserted into her abdomen following the removal of an inflamed appendix. I was at her bedside waiting for her to come round from the anaesthetic when into the ward strode the doctor who had administered it, still wearing his theatre garb. I was surprised, because the patient appeared to be recovering well from the minor operation.

It was not the patient he was interested in, but me. He asked if I was the nurse who had been in the theatre, because he had fallen in love with my eyes!

I was filled with confusion and trepidation and terrified that Sister Hyman would see this Dutch doctor flirting with me. Student nurses were strongly discouraged from any association with the medical staff, and usually, being the lowest of the low, we were not put in a position where any discouragement was needed.

I remember that we went out together only twice. Perhaps my eyes were the only attraction, because he told me he was engaged to a girl in Holland.

We were off duty one day a week and a half day on Sundays. Lights out was at 10 pm, and we were allowed to apply for the occasional late pass. The working hours were very demanding and social events played only a minor role. Lack of funds did not make it easier to pursue a social life, as our rate of pay had still only reached the dizzy heights of £9 a month. A six-weekly visit to the cinema or a morning coffee in one of the then-popular coffee bars was our main recreational activity. We worked a shift system on day duty, the twelve hours divided into three shifts of four hours, which could vary from day to day. One day we could have the morning off after 10 am until 2 pm, afternoon off from 2 pm to 6 pm or finish for the day at 6 pm, having been on duty since 7.30 am with meal times off in between.

Night duty was a straight twelve-hour shift with a one-hour break for a main meal at midnight. There were separate sleeping quarters for those nurses trying to sleep during the day in the nurse's home near the senior trained nurses' rooms. These were well away from the hustle and bustle of students slamming doors, singing and dancing along corridors, free for a few hours like children released from school at the end of the day.

The shared bathrooms were frequently occupied, long hot soaks easing weary bones and tired feet. There was one period when the baths all acquired a brown rim where the high water mark had reached. Home Sister Holmes was soon on the warpath, and she quickly detected the guilty culprits by the colour of their skin. It had become our practice to dissolve potassium magnesium crystals in the hot water to acquire an instant tan.

After three months I was transferred on to my second ward, which was the male surgical one. The atmosphere was entirely different to that of the female ward. It was generally noisier, with fewer flowers and lots of attempts to pinch nurses' bottoms. Days off and shifts were allocated by the ward sister, the list pinned on a notice board in her office at the beginning of each week.

The ward routine was similar to the previous surgical ward, except that urinals were easier to hand out than bedpans. I think there must have been several cases of constipation, because few pans were requested. It may have been the dreadful balls of brown tow which were used instead of toilet paper which put people off.

There was a fireplace at one end of the ward and grouped around it were wooden Windsor chairs, high backed with arms that were extremely comfortable for patients when they were first helped out of bed.

This ward was on the ground floor. On one side the windows looked out over a yard, but on the opposite side they bordered a corridor which led to the dining room. Half an hour after the day staff had come on duty, I noticed two staff nurses always positioned themselves near these windows, supposedly to talk to patients whose beds were on that side of the ward.

Curious as to why they found this to their advantage, I began to notice that they only moved away after a certain doctor had passed on his way to breakfast. He seemed to have the same effect on them when he entered to do his morning ward round, when they would immediately be there to assist him. Dr Bob Wittenoon was different from the usual housemen, because they kept their stethoscopes in their white coat pockets, but his hung around his neck. All the medics do that now, but then it was new and very cool. He wore casual clothes, open-toed sandals, used a cigarette holder and had a very distinct Australian accent.

One day, Sister Saul asked me to accompany Dr Wittenoon to examine a patient. The staff nurses had kept out of sight, probably because it was the patient's rear end with protruding piles that had to be studied. I gave him the examination tray, which included the essential rubber gloves and lubricant, folded down the patient's bed covers and made reassuring noises. I may have blushed slightly or even fluttered my eye lashes, but I did not expect this doctor to see me as anything more than a first-year student on the opposite side of the bed.

That evening while in the nurses' sitting room, I was surprised to be summoned to the telephone by an irate staff nurse who thought I had done something wrong, because there was a doctor on the phone. In fact it was Dr Wittenoon, and he wanted to ask me out on my next day off, having persuaded Sister to change my day off to the same as his.

This was very worrying, as Sister must now know that the most junior nurse on her ward was being chatted up by a doctor. I had only worked on her ward for a few days, and she might get the wrong impression. It could also mean a hard time for me from the other, more senior nursing staff.

I had doubts that Dr Wittenoon really knew which nurse I was, and kept describing myself to him. He was very persuasive and reassuring, saying that Sister was most obliging and had not hesitated to change my day off.

When the day arrived I was still not sure he'd got the right nurse, as in the meantime he had not made eye contact on the ward. I duly turned up in the yard next to the ward where he kept his baby Austin. Ambulant patients were leaning on window sills observing the goings-on of their off duty staff, another concern for me about the whole expedition.

I did not know what the day would entail until we arrived at a flying club near Southend, where he kept an Auster plane. It was such a relief that my tweed skirt and flat shoes were the correct dress for my first venture in an aircraft. We took off and soared thousands of feet above Essex under a perfectly clear blue sky, with wonderful views over the countryside to the Mersea estuary and over Dedham Vale - Constable country. What a first date!

It did not end there, because on the return journey I was told to change into some 'glad rags' - we were going up to Mayfair. This created a feeling of panic. What was I going to wear? I did not own any glad rags, but my friends had been waiting to hear all about my day and they soon rallied round. An unladdered pair of stockings was produced, together with a pair of pearl earrings from another friend. I searched my wardrobe and found a dress I had worn for a wedding, which I took to be ironed. A hot bath was run for me and my shoes were cleaned.

I abandoned the camel coat I had worn previously and put on a black one with a fur lining, which was supposed to add some glamour. My friends had also put make-up on me which was a new experience for me, especially the mascara, which I was unused to wearing. My eyelashes were thick and long, so I had not considered it necessary. I was concerned that it smelt like boot polish.

My escort had changed from casual pullover and slacks into a very smart tailored suit, white shirt and silk tie. He kissed my cheek when he opened the car door and looked suitably impressed.

The hour's drive to London, with butterflies churning in my stomach, was an outing in itself. We arrived in Berkeley Square (though I did not hear any nightingales singing!) and with no traffic or parking problems we entered the lush domains of the Colony nightclub. I was now well and truly out of my depth.

This was the beginning of a two-year whirlwind romance, with time spent together whenever our days off coincided, travelling the length and breadth of England and Wales, soaking up all the tourist sites and seeing them through the eyes of a visitor to this country. I discovered that Bob had connections in high places in the horse-racing world and a wealthy father in Australia. Most of all, he was a very compassionate and efficient surgeon whose patients liked and respected him. Unfortunately it all came to an end when he went to work in the Bahamas.

By then I was approaching my third and final year, and it was time to think about examinations. I had worked on several different wards, surgical, medical, orthopaedics, and I had 'practised' on both sexes all the treatments and procedures pertaining to their varying conditions. I had also spent time in the operating theatres, outpatient department and at our sister hospital Saint Johns, nursing on the gynaecological and paediatric wards.

My hectic social life had not interfered with my nursing, and as it had not intruded into the hospital it had passed unnoticed. I was fortunate that I had managed to keep off Matrons' carpet. My night duties were always on the private wing, where there were twenty-five single rooms off a long corridor.

My first experience on this ward during the first year of training was as a junior runner for a staff nurse whom I greatly admired. She was a tall, attractive girl with a Doris Day smile and a lovely disposition - my perfect role model.

I was amazed how daily at 6 am she was always full of energy and ready to tackle the demands of the next two hours - until she confessed that she took an amphetamine just before the mad rush of work began. I was encouraged to take one, and that was enough - never again. I had terrible palpitations and could not sleep during the day. I was hyperactive until it was time to return to the ward that evening. Following that experience I never again judged a book by its cover.

On this ward, one patient, an elderly woman who was supposedly bedridden, always had a pool of 'water' under her bed in the morning. When questioned about not ringing her bell to request a bedpan, she would reply, 'Oh, the cat's been in here again!'.

During my third year I was put on the same wing, but as the senior nurse in charge, with my own junior runner. I went to the first meal break at midnight, leaving the junior in charge. Returning after my meal and approaching the private ward corridor, I could see that a red light was on above one of the room doors. I quickly went to see what the patient needed and found a very upset man who informed me that someone had tried to get into his bed.

I then heard movement in an adjoining room - a room which was supposed to be unoccupied, according to the report which had been given to us at handover by the day staff. I nervously opened the door and was confronted by an apparition, naked apart from a white counterpane draped over one shoulder and trailing behind. It was the confused lady with pneumonia from another room.

Not knowing whether to laugh or cry, I escorted her back to her own room and her own bed and was very relieved that earlier in the evening a patient had not missed either a hot drink or any prescribed medication and that there really was a room which should have remained empty.

In the meantime I began to wonder why there was no sign of the junior nurse and why the bell had not been answered. She was not in the office where we sat when the patients were quiet, or in the sluice, so I decided to look in the other empty room, which had been prepared for an admission the next morning.

There I found my runner. Her cap was off and two young housemen were flirting with her. And the bed needed to be remade.

The doctors beat a very hasty retreat, hopefully to their own beds. A certain student had a very short meal break and was kept rushing around for the remainder of the night, firmly wearing her cap and not knowing if I would take the matter further with the powers that be. She also kept an eye firmly on the time during any further absences on my part.

The private wing was an interesting assignment, with a variety of medical and surgical patients. There was enough time to set very high standards of care, although with everyone behind closed doors vigilance was vital. In the small hours of the morning, when it was quiet, there was time to reflect on each person in our care, read through their medical notes and understand their anxieties.

I also enjoyed working on the gynaecological ward, which specialised in female ailments. Because these were the days before abortions were sanctioned, we did not have the added burden of nursing a woman who had chosen to have her foetus aborted next to a bed occupied by a woman who had desperately wanted her baby but had lost it through no fault of her own.

This experience made me aware of the psychological trauma these women endure, as well as the physical upset to their body chemistry. I would see the anguish on their faces, especially if they had been told that the baby was the gender they longed for and that there appeared nothing wrong with the tiny body.

The husbands often appeared bewildered by the female-dominated atmosphere and uncomfortable when trying to comfort their wives. I deliberately do not refer to them as 'partners', as it was unheard of then for a pregnant woman not to be wearing a ring on her left third finger. Single mothers were hidden away, as an illegitimate child was a disgrace to them and even worse for their families. Contraceptive pills were neither available nor imagined. Any 'hanky-panky' under or over the bed clothes was a game of roulette, depending on how responsible the man was. We had never imagined that females would eventually be able to control their own destinies by taking a daily pill.

There were also cases of simple D&Cs (dilatation and curettage), with just a few days of admission, a prolapsed uterus, often because of multiple pregnancies, and the more serious surgical intervention of a hysterectomy. It required special sensitivity to nurse all these patients. Perhaps that is why I found such satisfaction in it, and looking back wonder if maybe I should have specialised in 'gynae'.

Paediatrics might have been a straightforward placement for me after two years nursing children, but I found a completely different scenario in a general hospital compared with that of the long-term orthopaedic patients. The children were mostly acutely ill and there were many tiny babies just a few months old who required bottle feeding. This could take a considerable length of time when they were too weak to suck. It was heartbreaking to see parents leaving at the end of visiting time, when they needed to be with their offspring. It was my least favourite ward and I was pleased when the three months were completed.

Summoning up my thoughts and feelings towards the end of my three years, I began to consider how I should be directing my future and to which of the specialities I should be heading. I preferred surgical to medical nursing, as my time on a male medical ward had been spent mostly with diabetics, chest infections or heart cases. Coronary heart disease patients were nursed lying flat for several weeks, everything being done for the patient, who was supposed to not use any exertion. Diabetics often had leg ulcers, loss of sight or huge carbuncles on their necks, in their armpits or groins. I learned how to apply magnesium sulphate and kaolin poultices, how to test numerous urine specimens and measure and administer insulin dosages. Varicose leg ulcers were a challenge as there were no magic bullets, it was just a question of time spent cleaning and dressing these unpleasant and painful wounds. Never seeing a good result however much I tried to heal them was very frustrating.

There was no piped oxygen for the chest infections or asthmatics. It was given through a facial mask with a tube leading to a large oxygen cylinder, which had to be trundled to the bedside by a porter. This procedure made enough noise to awaken the whole ward. Very ill patients were given oxygen tents, which were erected around the top half of the bed. They encompassed it, making the patient difficult to nurse.

I recall the medical ward sister becoming extremely upset over one admission, a sixteen-year-old boy who died of uraemia. She blamed herself for not suggesting to the houseman that a blood specimen should be sent to the pathological laboratory to help diagnose this young man's illness. Sister O'Neil was very experienced and frequently pointed a young doctor in the right direction if he lacked experience.

On medical wards where there were more chronically-ill patients there were also more deaths, so one not only became familiar with the procedures for laying out the deceased but also with sitting with a patient during their last hours. Our patients never died alone. Day or night, a member of staff was always asked to sit with them, often in a side ward, or if on the main ward it was behind closed bed-curtains. If a relative was present they were given the privacy and support they needed. We made sure food and drinks were offered and that they understood the inevitable outcome. The bereaved were treated with respect and understanding.

My first experience of death was a middle-aged spinster who had no close relations. She clung to my hand for comfort as I sat with her before she lapsed into a coma. Death can be a lonely and agonising time, but I was fortunate as this lady had a deep faith and was welcoming her end. The ward sister asked me to help her lay out the body, which was done with great tenderness and reverence. Her hair was carefully brushed and arranged, her hands folded over her chest and a rose placed between them before the mortuary attendant arrived with a trolley covered by a purple cloth to take the body to the chapel of rest.

It was well known that the mortuary attendants were not always as respectful if a junior nurse had to accompany them with the body across the hospital grounds during the hours of darkness. They would play tricks by disappearing on some pretext before they reached the mortuary, leaving the nurse alone.

Once final examinations were behind me and I had obtained my registration with the General Nursing Council, I was able to wear a navy blue belt and be called Staff Nurse. Hearing those words was more meaningful than later hearing myself called Sister. At the time I was working on male orthopaedics, where there were several young men suffering from multiple fractures sustained during road traffic accidents, especially involving motor bikes. This was before the advent of compulsory safety helmets, and some of them had devastating head injuries which left them mentally damaged. Their behaviour was so disturbed that they had to be restrained and enclosed with bed boards to keep them in bed and prevent further injury to themselves or others.

Male orthopaedics was never quiet, but with a head injury patient on the ward it could be even noisier. If a patient was too fractious they would be given injections of paraldehyde, a foul-smelling solution which I disliked, especially as I did not like the effect it had on the patient, rendering them unconscious.

When I finished my first day on duty as a staff nurse, I crossed over from the ward to the nurses' home. On my way I was approached by the senior sister in charge of the operating theatres. She remembered me from my six months of operating theatre training, perhaps because during that time I scalded my hand. They used a very unsafe practice of removing sterilized instruments in a stainless steel basket from boiling water and balancing the basket on a wobbly trolley. I was doing exactly as instructed when the basket slipped on to my hand. I gritted my teeth and completed my journey to the operating table. Fortunately the anaesthetist was good at reading non verbal signs. He realised that I was in pain from the scalding and rushed me to casualty.

Being newly qualified, I was not ready to leave the patient's bedside, so I decided to apply for a staff nurse vacancy in a small unit away from the main hospital building. It catered for male and female

convalescent patients and where there was also a ward for genito-
urinary patients. I liked the atmosphere and the excellent ward sister.
On most days I accompanied the consultant in charge on his ward
round, and after I had been there a few months he asked Matron if
she would upgrade me to sister, so that I could replace one who was
leaving from another of his wards.

Matron was very reluctant to accept this idea, stating that she
thought I should work as a staff nurse for at least two years. This
decision made me restless and anxious to explore pastures new. Being
too young for promotion, I decided to look outside the NHS.

Chapter Four

OVERSEAS WITH THE QAS

That decision by the matron at the Chelmsford & Essex Hospital changed my life. I decided to apply to join the Queen Alexandra's Royal Army Nursing Corps, the nursing branch of the British Army. I really could not face remaining in the same hospital until I was old enough to become a sister, and certainly not a matron. Surely someone would marry me before then!

The interview was held in Millbank in London and the panel consisted of four 'Queen Bees' with the ranks of Colonels and a Brigadier. I was cross-examined for an hour about my work and social experiences, and then asked why I had only applied for a two-year short-service commission. This would mean postings would be no further than the UK or Germany.

For some unknown reason I had a yearning to go to Hong Kong, even though I had never read or seen anything about it or met anyone who had been there. So sitting behind a table with those four imposing females glaring at me, I changed my two-year enlistment to a four-year one, having been reassured that the Far East would become my destiny provided I first passed my medical examination.

This took place on the same day in the same building, and was conducted by two elderly retired RAMC Brigadiers. I was instructed to remove all my clothes apart from my pants. The examination consisted of no more than jumping up and down! With four candidates for interview that morning, if they all had the same examination as I did, I wondered what condition those two old fossils were in at the end of the day.

I was granted the four-year short service commission and preparations started almost immediately to turn me into an officer. Fittings with a London tailor were arranged to kit me out with an incredible number of uniforms for ward work, duty officer duties, parades and walking out.

The ward dress comprised dove-grey dresses with red epaulettes and red shoulder capes, both of which had the status symbol of two gold pips. There were red detachable cuffs and a large stiffly-starched cap with a red embroidered QA badge on the point, which hung down one's back. Black lace-up shoes completed the outfit, which was marred only by thick khaki stockings.

Our 'number 1 uniform' was a grey jacket and straight skirt and a stiff peaked cap. A more comfortable battle dress jacket and skirt were issued in khaki with a soft peaked cap. This was worn when you were Duty Officer, and during the six weeks at the training depot in Hindhead, Surrey.

During basic training we had lectures on military history, law and rank comparisons of the three services. The first thing we had to learn of course was our army number, followed by the various numbers of all the forms which had to be completed in triplicate.

Having been instructed on how to wear our uniforms, 'bull' our shoes and salute, we spent hours on the parade ground being drilled and instructed by a Sergeant Major who endeavoured to lick us into shape so that we could impress HRH Princess Margaret, the Corps Colonel, when she inspected our passing-out parade. It was the only time any of us were ever on parade. Looking at a photograph of myself in uniform with my cap too far back on my head, I now know why it blew off during the march past!

Each morning we were woken by an orderly at 6.30 with a cup of tea. I received mine first, being in room number one, and soon learned that if I woke up early enough and was cleaning my shoes when he knocked on my door, he would return and shine the toes after he had delivered tea to the remaining nineteen doors. This left me time to press my skirt and battledress top, the first of the twice-daily changes of uniform.

We usually had time off during the weekends, until one weekend when we were detailed to clean our barracks windows before the arrival of a visiting General. This came as a shock to all of us, as with our newly-acquired officer status we had got used to being saluted by all the other ranks when we went out of our way to pass a group of soldiers.

The only other escape from the camp was to the Punchbowl, an inn near the Hog's Back. It was several miles walk, but at our newly-acquired marching pace it did not take too long and the drink at the end of it was worth the effort.

The day arrived when the posting orders were issued and the twenty nurses in our group were distributed across the UK. Military hospitals were numerous then; I remember the Royal Herbert in Woolwich, the Cambridge and Louise Margaret in Aldershot, Netley in Southampton, Tidworth and Catterick in North Yorkshire, among the many. We were therefore scattered to the four winds, except that I managed to catch only a slight breeze and found myself walking across the road from the depot to the Connaught Hospital, the military chest centre.

The Connaught consisted of wooden hutted buildings with six wards and a large operating theatre, an RAMC mess and, well away from temptation on the opposite side of the site, a QARANC one.

We were not supposed to fraternize with the NCOs, so it was not considered important that their mess was next to ours. The female other-ranks barracks was in a very remote area, which made for a long trek when an orderly officer had to do the night rounds to make certain that they were all sleeping in their own beds.

My first ward was the one allocated to officer patients, usually managed by a major who was on long leave. I found that I had very little to do. The RAMC sergeant dished out duties to the orderlies while I distributed medication, gave injections, changed dressings and accompanied the CO on his ward rounds (apart from going into the latrines, which were out of bounds to females). I also worked out the staff off duties and tried to be pleasant to the patients, and of course to the MOs.

While I was on this ward I celebrated my 23rd birthday, and two of the orderlies arrived for duty carrying huge bunches of flowers. They were Sweet Williams, and I found out later they had completely denuded a neighbours' garden. I should have put them both on a charge, but I didn't know how to. I just hoped no one would put two and two together.

This easy number changed when the major returned and I was given my own ward. It comprised two separate wards, one on each side of the main corridor. On one side were the ENT patients, all male, and on the other were patients who had undergone chest surgery.

This is where I first became acquainted with Gurkha soldiers. These were patients who had been flown to the UK from the Far East to undergo major chest surgery to excise the scar tissue in their lungs which resulted from an attack of tuberculosis. Initially this had been treated with large doses of a combination of antibiotics to clear the infection.

They spoke no English, and were terrified of their strange surroundings and the unfamiliar operation that faced them. It was very disconcerting at the end of my first day on this ward, when the lights were out and I was doing my final ward round, to find a row of bodies with no heads. The bed covers were pulled up and tightly tucked under the backs of their heads so that they looked like a row of mummies. To check if their breathing was regular I had to watch the rise and fall of the bed covers, not having the courage or inclination to disturb the unknown.

It was a completely different experience when I entered the ward during the day. They would immediately lie at attention and hands together, greeting me in unison with 'Namaste Memsahib'. Little did I know that I was to hear this hundreds of times in the years ahead. I cannot remember even the youngest of these brave men complaining of pain or discomfort, grumbling at the food or trying to 'chat me up', quite unlike the remainder of my patients.

During my reorganisation of the ward facilities I made sure that the beds had at least two pillows, with sufficient extra ones in the walk-in airing cupboard, but I still had a hundred surplus pillows. I contacted the Quartermaster and suggested that they should be collected and put in the stores. Two privates arrived with a trolley on to which the pillows were piled and they trundled away with the load. Months later when I handed over the ward before my next posting, I was a hundred pillows short. I had not asked for the appropriate ABF104 (I think that's the correct number) which was the form required to prove that they were taken away and that I had not lost or stolen them.

The CO was not amused by this, any more than he was when he summoned me to explain why I had spent my off duty playing tennis with another rank. It was not considered appropriate, even though this National Service man had a degree from Cambridge and was an excellent tennis player. I was glad that we had not been spotted together at the local cinema by the two QA majors sitting in front of us.

My posting to Hong Kong was probably hastened when the

hospital pharmacist complained that I had relabelled all the ward medicine bottles. I had considered that the old ones were dirty and illegible and did not fit in with my spotless ward. Twenty years later when I read that he had become President of the Royal Pharmaceutical Society, I could not resist writing and telling him that he had done me a tremendous favour.

My transit to the 'fragrant harbour' (the original meaning of Hong Kong) was interrupted by a short spell on a ward in Aldershot. As I waited there for an available flight I was on continual standby and made several false starts, finally leaving for Brize Norton at very short notice.

The flight, if I remember correctly, was on a DC4. It took 24 hours with four stops, including one in Istanbul, when I experienced the indignity of having to use the holes in the ground which served as loos. You had to straddle them with your feet on the wet sides, trying to aim straight. On the journey I also tasted thick Turkish coffee and picked up a dose of Delhi belly.

Expecting to arrive in Hong Kong in the autumn, I had been advised to pack winter kit in my flight luggage and send my tropical kit in the heavy baggage which was going by sea. I wore a jersey wool dress and jacket for the journey, thinking it appropriate for a flight leaving from an autumnal UK and arriving during a cooler month in HK. How wrong can you be? When the plane finally reached its destination and the aircraft door opened, the heat overwhelmed me. It was like putting your head in an oven. I began to wonder why I hadn't simply remained a staff nurse.

In fact we had touched down in Singapore, not Hong Kong. I thought it must be another short stop, until I suddenly found myself bundled out of the airport and into a Land Rover by a very assertive QA driver who took me to the military hospital, where I was deposited on the steps of the sergeants' mess.

My pride once again dented, I began to realise how inadequate military communications can be, and that I had become a chattel rather than an individual. I did eventually arrive in the correct building and convinced the duty officer that although I was not expected, I was a QA sister.

By the time I had got used to sleeping enveloped in a mosquito net and putting up with the house lizards, the intense humidity, and the constant whirring of overhead fans, I was being detailed to pack and go to the docks to embark on a troop ship for Hong Kong.

On the docks, also waiting to embark, was a group of engineer officers from Butterworth in North Malaya, on their way for R&R leave. Having all made eye contact we expected a pleasant voyage, but the South China Sea had different ideas and for four days the SS Oxfordshire was buffeted non-stop by a tropical storm. None of us emerged from our cabins until we sailed in to Victoria harbour, having lain groaning with sea sickness throughout the journey.

I have never since been tempted to go on a cruise, and on reflection I wonder what attraction the Northumberland Fusilier Officers had that persuaded me to go sailing with them from the Hong Kong yacht club.

My first sight of Hong Kong was through an early morning mist. The island appeared out of a haze which heralded a warm day to follow. The harbour was alive with small vessels, sampans, wallah-wallahs and red-sailed junks. They appeared minute alongside the Star ferries and the Royal Navy and American warships berthed on both sides of the harbour.

After disembarking I was met by a QA major who escorted me across the water to the island in the motor launch used by the Commander British Forces, a very dignified start. Then there was a climb into a Land Rover, which proceeded up the winding road to the Peak, the highest point on the island. Halfway up we passed BMH Bowen Road, but as I was not midwifery trained, this was bypassed and I was taken further up through the jungle-covered hillside to

BMH Mount Kellett at the top, an ex-Royal Naval hospital which had just been taken over by the Army.

This was a very imposing building, with wide steps up to a huge main door. However I was not deposited here, but taken further along the road to a delightful house which was the QA sisters' mess. I was given a spacious ground-floor room with an adjoining bathroom. There was also a large and pleasant sitting room and an elegant dining room with a separate guest room, where we were able to entertain privately as often as we could.

The hospital was large and very busy with acute medical and surgical cases. In addition to the soldiers' wards there was a separate one for officers and families. Another ward was for men suffering from venereal diseases, which was strictly out of bounds to the sisters. Surely the powers to be did not think the infection was airborne?

My first placements were short spells on various wards, until I was asked if I would like to train for my Army Operating Certificate and transfer to theatres. This was a wonderful opportunity to escape from wards on which there were at least four sisters, the ones in charge being Majors who had been in the army so long that they were out of touch with modern methods. We were their handmaidens, and it was back to being nothing more than staff nurses. This rankled after I had been running my own wards.

Before transferring to theatres, I was on duty on the families ward when an undernourished five-year-old Nepalese child was admitted into my care. Her father had been home on long leave, during which his young wife had died. Recognising that his daughter was extremely ill and in pain, and he was at the end of his leave and had to return to the 1st Battalion 7th Gurkha Rifles, he carried her down from his hill village. The powers that be and local authorities turned a blind eye and her admittance into the colony was not questioned.

She was the sweetest child, and she must have been bewildered

Queen Alexandra's Royal Army Nursing Corps

Favourite hobby off duty

Training depot lieutenant

Ward sister

Connaught Army Chest Hospital,
Hindhead, Surrey

October 1959 - November 1960
Singapore to Hong Kong

South China Sea

British Military hospital, Mount Kellett, Hong Kong

Theatre Sister

Denis O'Leary

by all her new experiences, the strange surroundings, the alien language and the uniforms. She was in terrible pain and could not bear her own weight, so she required many investigations. I reassured her and remained with her throughout the numerous, lengthy medical tests. I tried to persuade her to take food, but she continuously rubbed her abdomen before retching and showing signs of vomiting. I rushed to get a large kidney dish, which was quickly filled with 35 fat round worms. The anti-parasitic medication given to her at admission had worked and destroyed these dreadful parasites. It was not surprising that she was malnourished.

Her medical diagnosis was not a primary worm infestation but tuberculosis of a hip joint. A course of streptomycin injections were begun and she never once complained, although the needle was a wide-bore one to allow the thick syrupy fluid to flow freely.

She was eventually discharged, grew up in the family lines, attended the school there and many years after being hospitalized, she married a rifleman in the battalion. I did see her when she was a young woman, looking very beautiful in her sari, and was delighted that I had played a small part in her recovery.

I may have inadvertently played a less significant role when looking after a tiny Nepalese baby. I asked if I could cut off the many pieces of string which were round the abdomen and wrists, having no knowledge of their religious significance. At that stage in my life, I was very keen to tidy and clean everything in sight. Perhaps that is why the operating theatres suited me.

Chapter Five

IN THEATRE

The two operating theatres were on the top floor of the hospital, and I shared the responsibility of working them with a Captain. Working opposite shifts, we covered the 24 hours. It was vital work as there were many emergency surgical interventions.

When I first entered the theatres I was struck by the clinically stark rooms and how organized the staff were, each member knowing exactly what their responsibilities were before and during the operations. It soon became evident how essential this methodical approach to detail was, especially when dealing with emergency admissions.

The other sister and I were ably supported by a team of RAMC privates who had been trained as theatre technicians. These were chaps doing their two years' National Service, and they had very diverse backgrounds. There was a carpenter, a plumber, an accountant and a farmhand. The accountant was Jewish and was always around for the circumcisions.

On my first night on call I heard a knock on my bedroom door at midnight. When on call for emergencies, like a mother I slept with one ear open, so I soon roused myself to ask what the emergency was. I was told that two troopers had been seriously burnt when their Centurion tank had exploded during a night exercise.

The two men had been treated at the scene of the accident by the military first aiders after they had been evacuated from the burning tank, at great risk to their lives from other members of their troop. They were then brought to the military hospital by an army ambulance, bumping along uneven roads the fifty miles from the Chinese border to the island, across the harbour by ferry and then to the top of the Peak and eventually to the hospital. It was a long and arduous journey, and although the deep burns had destroyed nerve endings they both also sustained surface burns, which were extremely painful.

I quickly put on my grey uniform dress and ward cape and made my way to the hospital. Instead of using the lift to the third floor I hurried up the flights of marble stairs. The antiquated lift clattered and clanged and I had no wish to awaken the sleeping ward patients.

On entering the theatre I could see that the technician had laid up the surgical trolley and everything was ready for the patients' arrival. I changed into the theatre dress and head scarf to conceal my hair and went into the scrub room where I scrubbed my hands and forearms meticulously. Unfolding the sterile gown, I slipped my arms into the sleeves. The medical orderly tied the tapes of the gown at the back while I put on the sterile surgical gloves, folding the cuffs carefully over the ends of the sleeves. The on-call surgeon was close behind me and scrubbed up while I checked the trolley contents. I opened several packs of dressings, swabs and extra sterile towels. From what I could ascertain it would be a cleaning-up procedure rather than open surgery.

The condition of the patients meant they were only sedated and not anaesthetised. The priority was to put up an infusion of saline, as the men were losing copious amounts of fluid. There were no obvious veins in which to insert the needle, which meant cutting down to find a vein. We first treated the less seriously burnt patient, the surgeon and I working in tandem to clean the burns with normal saline solution, the surgeon carefully removing the blackened dead skin.

The worst burns were over his trunk and legs; his face and arms were unscathed. Instead of covering them with dressings we decided he would be nursed exposed on sterile sheets. A bed was brought from the ward on to which he was transferred and then taken to a side ward which had been prepared by the night staff.

The next lad had second and third degree burns that were covered in black oil and we had to replace some fluid before commencing the big clean up. We worked tirelessly through the night, trying to cause as little discomfort to the patient as we could while ensuring he was sufficiently sedated to keep him still. It was demanding work and at the time appeared to be an endless task of gentle cleaning, swabbing and removing dead skin.

At last it was time for the soldier to join his mate and the attentive ward staff who would keep them free from infection by using barrier nursing techniques in a dust-free environment. It took several weeks of this attention before these brave young men could be evacuated back to the UK, where they would undergo plastic surgery. In the heat and humidity of the sub tropics it was due to good nursing that neither of them suffered any infections and their prognosis was good.

There was another night time occasion when we treated an amputation. A gunner had had his arm ripped off because he had stuck it out of a speeding truck window.

There were burst appendices, ruptured hernias and bleeding and perforated gastric ulcers. There were also routine hernias to be repaired, varicose veins to be stripped, football-damaged knees to be investigated, tonsillectomies and a few circumcisions to be snipped. Complicated fractured limbs occurred mostly from rugby injuries, as the ground played on was baked solid.

On the alternate nights when I was on call for emergencies, the technician on duty would lay up the surgical instrument trolleys and prepare the theatre before waking me. I would then arrive in the theatre just before the patient, in time to scrub up ready to assist the surgeon. This system worked well until in the early hours of one morning I was called to help with a perforated gastric ulcer. This is a major procedure requiring prompt intervention.

The surgeon made the skin incision while I checked my instruments, only to discover that the two large abdominal retractors were missing from my trolley. These were needed to pull and hold back the abdominal muscles so the surgeon could repair the perforation with a 'purse string stitch'. The retractors which I needed had been borrowed by the other hospital. There was no time to retrieve them, so with shorter and narrower retractors I endeavoured to assist the Colonel. He never referred to this but carried on as if my hands were not in his way. He had served in the army long enough not to be fazed by improvisations.

After a night assisting with emergencies, it was not worth trying to get any sleep before coming back on duty for the routine morning theatre cases. I would take my time scrubbing all the surgical instruments which had been placed in a deep porcelain sink from where I could enjoy the view through a window where far below down the hillside was a tiny fishing village called Aberdeen. I could watch the fishing vessels return in the dawn from their night's activities, slowly returning across the sea with their lights flickering, ready to offload their catch of lobsters and prawns to the floating restaurants with their red roofs, dragons on each corner and hanging lanterns with red and gold fringes swinging with the gentle movements of the boats. These were magical moments

While I was working in theatres the colony was hit by Typhoon Mary. Typhoons were always called by female names starting at the beginning of the alphabet at each new year. Everything was battened down, shutters were placed across windows and doors were virtually barricaded. One of the theatre windows cracked and exploded on to the ground below, fortunately with no injuries apart from a few racing hearts.

The only other casualty was a patient who absconded from a ward, a British officer called Major Denis O'Leary from the 1st Battalion 7th Gurkha Rifles, who had decided to go 'walkabout'. He was missing for quite a long time, causing the ward sister some anxious moments. She was still fuming over dinner in the mess that evening, not understanding how anyone could walk anywhere against a 100 mph wind. I suspect he did not walk at all, but was on his hands and knees.

I next met the Major when he was duty officer and came to the hospital to visit a Queens Gurkha officer, Lieutenant Indrabahadur Rai, a patient on the ward where I had based myself, as I too, was duty officer. At the time I was sitting at a desk, talking to three medical officers who were all standing. There was probably a lot of flirting, but I am sure it was not on my part!

Major O'Leary approached my desk and asked if he could see the QGO. I pointed him in the right direction. The MOs were standing and could see the major's crown on his shoulder, but I, sitting down, could not, and omitted to call him Sir. As he turned away to follow my directions, one of the doctors gave me a nudge, pointing out his rank. I quickly jumped up and went to escort him to see the patient, at the same time amending the way I addressed him.

I had not realised that in making this simple act of etiquette correction I had begun the first step towards marriage.

It was the beginning of a whirlwind romance. For Denis it entailed a regular bicycle ride all the way from Dills Corner in the New Territories to Fanling railway station, a train to Kowloon, the Star ferry across the harbour, a run to the funicular tram to the Peak terminal and then a taxi to the QA mess. When he insisted on making this arduous return journey several times a week, I had no option but to accept his proposal. In any case I was mesmerized by those stiffly starched uniform shorts, which could stand up on their own.

This may have also come about because based at the hospital main reception desk was a clerk on attachment from 1st/7th GR who acted as a translator. He had seen an OC from the same battalion hanging around the hospital when I came off duty. He suggested that I should tell this OC something in Gurkhali (at the time I knew only a few words like namaste, nani, didi, bhaini and bemar cha ki?), but his suggestion was 'Ma tapain laiya maya garchu'. (I am in love with you). He could have told me to issue an invitation to anything from a ball to a boxing match, for all I knew.

The news of my engagement to a Gurkha Major quickly found its way around the nursing corps, and the general opinion was that they always thought I would do something like that! I am sure to this day that many of my ex-colleagues think I am wearing a sari and living in the Himalayas.

Introductions to the battalion during the ensuring few months reassured me that I was to become part of a very close-knit community. I had to relinquish my commission on the day of our wedding, there being no other option in the days before it was recognised as sex discrimination! Just one year after I had arrived in Hong Kong we had a real battalion family wedding, with friends and colleagues supporting us and more than compensating for the absence of our own families who were not able to travel from the UK.

The Gurkha officers who had formed the Guard of Honour gave us a wedding kukri, a traditional Nepalese knife, and pinned a gold regimental badge on to my wedding dress, the first one made in the lines after the Battalion had become the Duke Of Edinburgh's Own.

I was given away by the Commanding Officer. Everything was timed to perfection, with the best man in charge of the meticulous arrangements. Sitting in the car on the way to the church in Fanling, I was very conscious that a beady eye was on the CO's watch to ensure that my arrival was precisely two minutes late. That day Battalion Part One orders had been issued with the exact timings and responsibilities for all to obey!

So I began my new life as the wife of an army officer, becoming acquainted with the Gurkha families when visiting them in the family lines, seeing their children at school and the new mothers in the Regimental hospital. I was to remain in the Far East for ten years, with long leave at three-year intervals, until 1969 when we returned to the UK. During our time in the Far East we lived in north and south Malaya before it became part of Malaysia.

It was a time of conflict in Borneo, so Denis was frequently there on active service with his regiment. He came home for two weeks' rest and recuperation every three months. I was fortunately spared the information about the fighting in the jungle, and only realized how dangerous it had been when my husband was awarded a bar to the military cross he had earned in Burma twenty years before.

The time spent apart passed quickly for both of us. I was busy with our young family, having given birth to a son in Hong Kong and three daughters in Malaya, and with numerous house moves to army quarters in the two countries.

The last three years before we returned to the UK was back in the Crown Colony of Hong Kong, when Denis was promoted to Lieutenant Colonel. With British Nanny Evelyn to assist with the children and Chinese house servants taking care of domestic chores, I assumed the role of the Colonel's lady. It was not one of leisure but involved helping to host numerous occasions in the Battalion and our quarter. There were several VIP house guests. We were wined and dined extensively by other regiments, Royal Navy and Royal Air Force personnel, civilian police and civil servants at dinner parties including Government House.

During the 1960s there was a craze for dressing-up parties and we toddled along in romper suits to a teachers' play-pen party, wore nuns' and monks' habits and attended a 'saints and sinners' party hand in hand. Then there was one where harem veils were appropriate.

**Wedding Day -
November 4th 1960**

Fanling
New Territories,
Hong Kong

Our first home

Ahcheun Fau Wong

Ah Sheung

1966

Buckingham Palace investiture

Husband Denis receives the Bar to his Military Cross (1966)
for operations in Borneo. With our son Timothy and daughter Jane.

1966 - 1969

Farewell to the Gurkha families - March 1969

Saints & Sinners party
- another hat

The more sedate dinner invitations to places like Government House were very grand occasions and a wonderful opportunity to wear our best evening clothes. Hats had an airing for Garden parties and presenting trophies on sports and swimming gala days.

To keep the adrenalin flowing with fewer social gatherings in 1967, there were threats from the Chinese army, which was massing on the border of the Colony. My husband's battalion were deployed to patrol the vulnerable area and keep the situation calm. I had been instructed to have passports and essential emergency supplies near at hand and to be ready to evacuate the home if my husband sent a Gurkha rifleman to warn me that the danger had escalated. It was fortunate that I never had to walk eight miles through the hills with four small children to Sek Kong, the Army village, to find sanctuary.

In 1969 when Denis finally had a posting in the UK and we settled not into an army quarter but into our own home in Suffolk, another daughter was born. The older children were settled into schools and I was able to think once again about returning to nursing, perhaps earlier than I expected when our GP visited our home to see our youngest girl who had croup. He asked me if I would like to work as a part-time practice nurse in the local surgery, and also in the RAF medical centre, where he held a twice-weekly clinic for the air force families. It was an opportunity to put on uniform again and find my other self.

Chapter Six

PRACTICE NURSE

Wearing the navy blue dress of a qualified nurse, silver buckled belt and white starched cap, I drove to the medical centre for the RAF families' clinic where I was to work. As I arrived at the main gate into the camp my car was halted by the guard, who asked me to present my credentials at the guard house while he opened my car boot and bonnet to search for any 'bombs'. Having an Irish surname, I was immediately suspected of having undesirable acquaintances, and recently there had been some IRA activity in the UK.

Having convinced them of my innocence, I was pointed in the direction of the medical centre. Here there were already several wives and children in the waiting area and a very distinct scent of exotic fragrances. I had not realized that the doctor who had employed me was so attractive to the opposite sex, but there was no doubt that the smart outfits, newly-set hair and carefully-applied make up were to impress someone, and I was sure it was not their new nurse.

The work was not demanding. It comprised injections, usually for vaccinations or inoculations before a wife accompanied a husband on a posting abroad. There were a few wounds to be dressed, prescriptions to be dispensed and routine cervical smears and specimens to be sent to the local district hospital.

That was, until I became aware of the frequent return appointments made by one or two of the wives. There were no apparent reasons for them to have repeat breast examinations, and I suggested to the doctor that it would be wise if I chaperoned them during their next visit. I do not think he realized what position he had been put in, and had no idea that he could be compromised. Once the doctor had me in attendance our caseload decreased considerably, and we saw only patients who were in genuine need of medical attention.

Working in the main practice surgery with three general practitioners was not demanding, and there was not sufficient nursing for any job satisfaction. I was not interested in filling in time answering the telephone, making patients' appointments and getting out case notes for the next sessions, eroding the receptionist's role, nor dispensing medication following patient consultations with the doctor.

It became even more irksome after one busy morning helping the dispenser when she inadvertently dispensed the wrong tablets and then accused me of the mistake. Reading prescriptions was an art in itself and I did enjoy deciphering the challenge. To this day I never have any difficulty reading the most appalling scrawl.

I also found that the youngest partner would discuss her patients with the other staff in a detrimental manner, forgetting about confidentiality with her wink wink, nudge nudge innuendos.

It was time to move on, and as our youngest daughter was now in full-time schooling and the other offspring were all at boarding schools, I decided I could work longer hours. When I saw an advertisement for a trained nurse to set up an occupational health department in a food factory, I applied, and got the job.

Chapter Seven

CHOICE CUTS

The factory was called Farm Kitchen Foods, in the village of Elmswell near Stowmarket. On my first day I was taken out to the yard and shown a static caravan where I was to administer whatever care was required. Inside there was very little equipment, a few dressings, nothing sterile and some out-of-date instruments for ear syringing and taking blood pressures or temperatures. There were no patients' records and no table or examination couch on which patients could lie.

Factory geography was unknown territory, but before I could decide where to find the equivalent of a quartermaster, I saw a line of men beginning to queue outside my new domain. I opened the door and asked if any of them was in urgent need of treatment, as I needed to get some equipment before I could efficiently help anyone. They had all just come to have a look at the nurse, but I used their help to point me in the direction of the stores' manager (and not to the pig procurement man, which one clever oaf tried to convince me was the right direction).

The store man had a supply of blue plasters, which he told me I would be using in abundance when all the butchers tried to cut off their fingers but very little else. He asked me to make a list and said he would supply my every need before the end of the day. He kept his word, though it was only nursing equipment and nothing personal he was talking about.

My next visit was to the carpenter's workshop, where I found a very helpful chippie and requested that he made me a surface on which I could dress upper limb injuries, somewhere I could suture all the promised cuts. He obliged me without delay.

Everyone so far was being remarkably helpful and responding immediately. The reason soon came to light when I learned that there was to be an inspection by a team from Marks & Spencer, as a contract was being negotiated with them.

The caravan was given a thorough clean, and a visit to the administration office ensured that it would be cleaned on a daily basis in the evenings when staff came in to clean the offices. I found my sister's uniform produced rapid results, as everyone was in awe of the hustle and bustle of starch.

I began to treat major and minor injuries, the worst being a deep groin cut when a butcher had failed to wear his protective leather apron. He was lucky that he had not cut the femoral artery, and I became aware of the need to instill some health and safety rules.

I was working an eight-hour day, but there were production lines operating during the evening and night so it was important that on each shift there was at least one first aider. I asked for volunteers and had a good response from some men and women. I selected the ones with some previous experience in the Scouts, Girl Guides or Red Cross cadets if they had done nothing more recent, preferably as a paramedic. However they were keen to learn and I instructed them in basic first aid, remembering the three Bs - breathing, bleeding and breakages.

In addition to the cuts there were headaches, period pains and malingerers, but it really was action stations when an overweight slaughter man had a major cardiac attack. Cardiac massage and the prompt arrival of an ambulance saved his life.

It was not possible to be bored here. Every day was different, and the first three months were hectic. One morning there was a knock on the caravan door. I was expecting another suture case or a cup of tea to console someone who had just been disciplined for a misdemeanour (by then the word had got round that I either had broad shoulders or I was a soft touch). In fact it was one of the company directors, which took me completely by surprise. He looked perfectly healthy in fact he was extremely young, handsome and debonair. There was nothing wrong with his well-being except for a concern over replacing the Personnel Manager, who had just handed in her notice.

He asked if I would take over the position. My initial reaction was to ask him what 'personnel' meant, but the salary was attractive, the hours were flexible and I liked the idea of yet another challenge. So I had a change of career.

I took to it like a duck to water. I enjoyed the organization, the writing and issuing of contracts of employment, the conditions of service, and above all the interviewing and selection of new employees. It all seemed to be based on common sense and a liking and understanding of people.

In order to know what was required in each department, I donned an overall, boots and a hairnet and went on to the factory floor, visiting each area from the slaughter house to the bacon and pork processing rooms. I even tried my hand at sausage making, much to the hilarity of all the observers on the production line. I then felt that I could justify the job descriptions that I was issuing.

In the meantime, to ensure ongoing medical care, I persuaded the powers that be to exchange the first-aid caravan for a portable cabin, in a better situation with easy access. This was staffed around the clock by trained first aiders. It did not require a registered nurse, so the budget was put to better use.

I thoroughly enjoyed my personnel management. Doesn't that

sound better than 'human resources'? I can never understand this ridiculous obsession with so called political correctness, what is so correct about 'human resources'?

I met people from all walks of life, encouraged the employment of disabled or physically-challenged personnel and re-educated some production managers into thinking about profound deafness being a handicap when packing bacon slices.

Chapter Eight

ON THE DISTRICT

I soon realised that my role as the tweed-suited woman with a briefcase who negotiated pay and conditions with union representatives and senior management did not sit comfortably with my spouse. Much as I liked being 'pig in the middle' (an imperative skill being to remain objective and keep a balanced viewpoint), I wondered, after four years, if I should once again be looking for the nurse in me. So when a vacancy for District Nursing Sister became available with West Norfolk Health Authority, I decided to apply.

Until I was appointed, the role had been filled by the local midwife, who had triple responsibilities. She also looked after district nursing and health visitor duties. This had been changed to make the service more efficient. Three separate posts were created, but with much larger geographical areas to cover.

I was interviewed in Kings Lynn by a senior nursing officer and her deputy. The SNO was elderly and was not in uniform, but had a very sour face. The deputy was a much younger version of her boss; she was the one I would have to report to if I got the job.

They were blessed with neither social graces nor interviewing skills, and seemed unprofessional and out of their depth. They must have been intimidated by my CV, not usually having to cross-examine an experienced human resources manager. It showed me that although nurses had been given managerial responsibilities in the

1970's they had not been given management training. I'm sure they struggled with offering me the position, but could find no reason not to. There were no other applicants, perhaps because other people were more aware than I was of what the work entailed.

During our half-hour chat they sat firmly installed behind a large desk, sitting on chairs higher than my own, which was placed so that the sun was in my eyes. If I had been questioned properly they could have been warned about my shortcomings. If they had been experienced interviewers, they would have known from my application form that I had no recent, up-to-date medical knowledge.

I had one week's useful induction with a very experienced Queens' district nursing sister called Sister Fox in the small town of Downham Market where she was based, which was also where we obtained our uniforms and equipment. She taught me that on entering a patient's house I should remove my coat and fold it inside out. I did not agree with that, though I didn't say so. It seemed to me more logical to keep the lining clean and uncontaminated by the often less-than-clean houses on our rounds. But during that first week I obeyed her instructions and tried to absorb as much information as she could impart before being let loose on my own patients.

My own area was around the Norfolk/Suffolk border, looking after the patients registered with two surgeries which had seven GPs between them. The oldest doctor, a lovely old darling who made each patient feel as if they were the only ones he had to see. There was also a middle-aged refugee who had returned to England from what had been Rhodesia when Mugabe took over. He had been a surgeon there and knew very little about diagnosing medical conditions.

The other doctors were all ages in between, and of mixed abilities. The youngest was a newly-qualified young female who had an inflated ego. She was very sarcastic and treated district nurses as if we were still on bicycles and only proficient at doing bed baths. She had a lot to learn, especially about useful techniques when it came to human relationships.

My cynicism of doctors started with her. Gone were the days when I had put them on a pedestal. I acquired a thicker skin and never felt intimidated by any of them again.

My duties covered five villages, numerous hamlets in between them and individual cottages tucked down long forest tracks. The handover from the previous nurse, who had worked in the area for twenty years, was a non-event. I was handed a pile of patients' records which were incomplete, tatty and dirty and had obviously shared a car with her dog.

A few patients were introduced to me, and it became obvious that their expectations were limited. They had become used to a rapid visit from the nurse, with little if any care being administered. This was to my advantage as I could be a new broom, with no role to live up to.

My only handicap was my husband, who was responsible for several local civilians who worked for the MoD. The first words spoken to me by my first patient were 'Oh, you're the Colonel's wife!' 'No' I replied, 'He is the district sister's husband'. That established the tone. Word soon got round that I did not see myself above them socially but was there to do a job and not play at being the benevolent lady.

It did not take me long to sort out the priorities. I acquired a large black bag to hold dressing packs and other nursing paraphernalia, and a smaller one to hold all the necessities for administering injections. Some of the nursing practices I had witnessed were poor - I had seen a syringe packet put into a pocket to give one lady her insulin - and there was no way I was going to have such low standards. I placed a clean sheet over the inside of my car boot to cover it, as I had collected piles of incontinent sheets and pads from the nursing stores. Perhaps I had a hangover from many years earlier, when I had been an Army theatre sister and everything was meticulous.

CHAPTER EIGHT

The health authority had replaced my Mini with a small Renault, as the Mini was not big enough for my very long body and legs, though anything was better than a bicycle. So it was that with my four wheels, my equipment, a willing heart and the joy of ignorance, I set off on the first round of my 'estate'.

Beginning my day at the furthest point from home, I planned to visit the patients in one village at a time, with hopefully no backtracking. It felt strange to be in a navy blue uniform dress with long sleeves which I never had the chance to unroll. They were tidily rolled up with white frilly cuffs, a navy blue overcoat and a pillbox hat, which someone described as a 'Jackie Kennedy'. Black tights and shoes completed the outfit, which served all seasons. I soon learned to put wellington boots in the car, along with several plastic carrier bags, piles of old newspapers, a blanket and a shovel together with a flask of something hot in the winter.

As I approached the first patient's house I realised how much one could guess from the outside what the circumstances were within. The garden needed some tender loving care, and the once-manicured lawn was like a wild meadow. The shrubs needed a haircut and the paintwork was flaking.

Sure enough, the elderly lady awaiting my ministrations needed the same attention. I tested her urine and gave her the correct dose of insulin, reassuring her that I knew exactly what I was doing, although it had been sixteen years since I had last looked after a diabetic patient. I did ask myself if I was really capable of carrying out this duty, but in for a penny, in for a pound, and I drove onwards to the next victim.

In later years I too became a diabetic, and I now have a greater understanding of why that lady always had high levels of sugar in her morning urine samples. She always had a large bowl of fruit salad for breakfast, not sticking to the advised hard apple or porridge. I could now assist her so much better.

The next elderly infirm patient had a very large, deep varicose ulcer. He had worked as a forester, and told me his leg was a mess because of working in damp thick undergrowth. He would arrive home at the end of each day with soggy calves (his own lower limbs, not junior bovines). I took off the bandages and was appalled at the size and discolouration of the ulcer. It looked as if it would never heal.

First things first. I cleaned it and covered it with a soothing and sterile dressing. Then I was able to show off my expert bandaging ability. When I first started nursing on leaving school, I trained in orthopaedics and learned that applying crepe bandages to hold splints was an important aspect of nursing. They were to support limbs damaged by infection or injury. We learned to apply bandages of differing patterns depending on their function, such as spiral, spica and double reverse spica, each turn being exactly the same width as the previous and following ones. At last I knew I had not forgotten everything I had learned all those years earlier.

The day continued, until I looked at my fob watch to be horrified at how quickly the time was flying by. There were still ten patients to visit and they were scattered throughout my patch.

I decided next to go and give a vitamin B injection, prescribed for a lady with shingles. I thought this would be a quick in-and-out call. I had not reckoned on the fury of the woman's husband, who thought I should have been there earlier. As I listened to a tirade of verbal abuse, biting my tongue and not attempting to justify my lassitude, I pulled myself up to my full height, putting on my Colonel's wife's voice (I knew it would come in useful at some time, only wishing that I had practised it more), and asked to see his wife. I proceeded to give her the injection and prepared to make my escape.

He thought the vitamin jab would immediately alleviate her suffering (shingles is extremely painful as it follows the nerve sheath), so he was even more irate when there was no immediate change. The next half hour was taken up explaining to him the nature of the herpes zoster virus, disillusioning him about the idea of a magic bullet bringing about a speedy cure and apologising for not being a miracle worker.

Following that visit, I desperately needed a calm atmosphere to regain my composure. I looked down my list for a straightforward case. A young autistic teenage girl required an enema to clear out her bowels, so I went there next. Good basic care would bring everything back into perspective.

I was met at the door by her father, who explained that his wife had gone away for a few days to recharge her batteries. The girl was in bed, and after introducing myself and telling her what was about to happen I started inserting the enema. This was a simple procedure, unlike the old days of a rubber tube, soapy water and a bucket.

She was very cooperative and easy to manage, but there was a lingering smell of semen around her groins and she had a 'cat that has stolen the cream' look on her face. Her father looked satisfied as well. This was a dilemma no textbook can help you with. I asked how often her mother went away, ascertained that her menstrual cycle was regular and then blanket-bathed her, paying special attention to the area between her legs and searching for any sign of a forced entry. There was nothing to suggest that she had been unwilling, no bruising, swelling or redness.

Going on my way, deep in troubled thought, I was not sure how to proceed. I did not know if I could take responsibility for the morality of this family, or if the girl was really being abused when she appeared so happy. How could I be the person to rock this family's boat? I decided to sleep on it.

My next patient was a person of whom I was to become extremely fond. Joan was in her fifties and had been a paraplegic for thirty years, having had a climbing accident on her honeymoon when she had fractured a thoracic vertebra. She cheerfully called out to me to enter the bungalow and told me where to find her.

The visit was to assist her into a bath, and had been a routine undertaken for several years, twice a week. It was against all the rules, which had been happily ignored. There was no hoist, so it was sheer muscle-power on the patient's part which made the operation successful. Having watched how she catheterized herself and did a manual evacuation of her bowels, I then lifted and guided her legs as she swung herself from bed into wheelchair. I pushed her through into the bathroom and after running the water and testing the temperature with my elbow (which I remembered having done before putting my babies into their baths), I again lifted and guided her legs into the bath. She swung herself over by leaning across to hold on to the far side. Her upper body strength was amazing, yet she looked all skin and bone.

We did the same in reverse order after I had washed her back and feet. She tackled the remainder, while I sat on the loo seat. Several years later this experience was to come in very useful when the youngest of our daughters suffered a similar fracture.

I confided to my patient what I had just witnessed, not being able to conceal my concern from this very discerning lady. I mentioned no names nor the village in which she lived, being very aware of patient confidentiality. Her advice was to leave well alone, but to have a discreet word with the father about the use of a condom. Joan said, 'Who knows, it may be the only sexual experience the girl will ever have, and even though she is autistic, why should not she have the pleasure?'

It was by now eleven o'clock and she offered me a coffee, but not knowing the state of the lavatories in the houses ahead, I declined and made my way to another village. The day had been anything but straightforward and uneventful, and I had yet to call into the surgeries to see if the doctors had added to my list, so I made my way there, delayed en route by the closure of a level crossing. It was clearly important to get a timetable to try and avoid future hold-ups here, as I would need to visit the surgeries frequently, if not to add to my list but to build up relationships with the staff. I hoped the GPs fully understood the new role I was trying to fill, and would not expect me to turn up for imminent births, visit schools to offer advice on health and hygiene or take antenatal classes.

I was spared the added burden of additional cases, but was given a mug of coffee and shown the staff lavatory before setting off to my next patient. This person lived down an unidentified forest track, initially difficult to find with no 'sat nav' to guide me and my ordnance survey map not helping. I eventually found the correct rutted track between rows of pine trees, bumping over uneven ground and not daring to go very fast. I had no idea how to change a wheel, which should really be an essential lesson for any district nurse!

Eventually I arrived at a flint cottage, one of a pair at least one and a half miles from the main road. The first cottage was derelict and the adjoining one appeared deserted among a forest - not of trees but of old cars. There were rows of them stacked high, surrounding and covering every square foot of ground.

I found my way to the side door, which was hanging off its hinges, knocked loudly and was eventually admitted into the scullery by a middle-aged woman with a dirty bandage on her lower leg. She was delighted to see me and offered to take some car batteries off the table and sit on one with her leg up on another so that I could redress the leg. Not surprisingly the injury had occurred when she had banged it on a spare car part. I changed the dressing, padding it well to avoid further injury. She then insisted that I went upstairs to see her mother.

I fought my way through piles of magazines, newspapers and bags of clothes which covered the room floor next to the scullery. It could not be called a sitting room, as there were no chairs and the floor was invisible under years of accumulated rubbish. I came to the stairs, which had become the overflow for yet more 'keepsakes'. There was about a six-inch space up the centre where I could slot my feet.

The mother was a frail ninety-year-old who was confined to bed. This was not because she was too infirm to get out of bed, but because she had lost the incentive to battle with her daughter's squirrel-like habits. Her large wrought iron bed was covered in a patchwork quilt and her mop cap covered snowy white curls. She looked as snug as a bird in a nest and I certainly was not going to ruffle her feathers by interrupting her life. I did however ask her offspring to fill a large earthenware jug with warm water, and proceeded to show her how to help her mother to what I hoped would become a daily toilet routine. Her dentures were in dire need of a toothbrush and her curls needed a good brush.

Shortly after I stopped visiting this remote cottage, as nursing requirements were no longer needed, these two females were raided by men who tied them up before searching the home for money. I am so relieved that I did not get caught up in that episode!

Finding my way back on to the main road, I realised that it was well past lunchtime, but that I could not possibly find time to go home even for a few minutes as I was only half way through my round. I passed a village shop and bought a small pork pie and an apple, which I trusted would stop my stomach from complaining as I drove onwards to my next adventure. I was beginning to have serious doubts about my change of occupation and wondered if I could retain a sense of humour against what appeared to be an unceasing series of setbacks, all preventing me from completing my planned day.

The remainder of my first day brought me into contact with the rear end of a young man who had a rectal sinus which needed packing with a glycerine gauze wick, some sutures for removal from an inguinal hernia (holding my breath against the unpleasant odour from an unwashed body) and visiting a bereaved widow whose husband had died a few days previously. We shared a comforting cup of tea as I listened to her relating the agony of his final hours. This experience left me emotionally drained, and with a deep longing for the physical energy I knew I would need to get through even busier days in the following weeks, months or possibly years.

Returning home I had to drive past the turning to a small church enclosed in a screen of pine trees set down a rough track in the forest. I had heard on the grapevine that a new priest had taken up residence in the presbytery of Our Lady of Consolation and Saint Stephen. As we were his nearest neighbours, even though we were a mile away, I felt that I should go and welcome him.

On pulling the bell chain the door was promptly opened and a tall Franciscan priest warmly welcomed me into his very basic home. He had been sitting pondering about his future. The presbytery had previously been occupied by an octogenarian priest and there had been no refurbishment of the house for fifty years. It was a terrible culture shock for this young American who had arrived to minister to our spiritual needs. He had begun to wonder about his next move.

Until some living improvements could be planned it seemed advisable to ensure that he had a meal and clean bed linen so that he could rest after his long journey. We immediately became friends, and in time he became my main supporter and mentor. Nursing on the district was very isolating, and with no support network I needed someone to whom I could offload the burden of coping with some very difficult situations.

My first day on the district was coming to an end, and it was soon time to put on my other hat and become a wife and mother again, switching off from other people's burdens and preparing a meal for five growing children. My fingers were crossed very firmly that there would be no calls on the answering machine at home from doctors, fellow nurses or patients which could not wait until the next day, and certainly not needing attention during the night.

A high level of nursing care was required, as I was soon to find that many of the patients were terminally ill. This was before Macmillan and Marie Curie nurses were established, so on the district we were responsible for the nursing care throughout the 24 hours. This meant visiting patients during the night to administer morphine injections when required, in addition to all the day treatments. What a blessing syringe drivers were when they arrived in later years, allowing patients to have a steady flow of pain-control medication.

When the sister covering the adjoining area had her days off I had also to do her caseload, which meant covering another five villages and yet more GPs (I don't mean covering them in the equine sense – I lived in Newmarket at one time and was well aware of the word's other meaning!). This meant accepting any referred patients. There were also times during annual leave when there would be two further areas to look after. It often meant driving more than 70 miles a day.

The work was arduous with little respite, but because of its nature it was extremely rewarding emotionally. The job satisfaction was very high, and I enjoyed meeting and looking after these brave, uncomplaining people. The bereaved families also needed support when the patient had died.

During this period, three incidents which left a very strong impression on me occurred within a month of each other. I attended three deaths, witnessing two of them, but the third had occurred several hours before my arrival in tragic circumstances.

The first death was of an elderly Anglo-Indian housekeeper who was an asthmatic. She lived in a presbytery near our home and looked after my friend the Franciscan priest. While she was cooking the supper, a pan of oil caught fire and set the kitchen alight. In a shocked state she tried to run up stairs to collect her inhaler and collapsed from heart failure. I was summoned by a visiting nun, but although a fire officer had tried resuscitation her heart was too weak to do more than flutter for a few seconds. I sat with her awaiting the GP. After twenty minutes I knew that her spirit had left her body. I did not see it, but her face changed and she looked very tranquil. A wonderful atmosphere surrounded her and I was filled with a deep feeling of peace.

A similar feeling came to me when I was with a male patient with terminal cancer. It suited him if I attended to him at midday, but one morning when I was in another village I had a strong sense that his wife was calling me. I drove to their house immediately and found her on their doorstep. She had willed me to arrive earlier than usual as she felt her husband was approaching the end of his life.

He was not comatose or breathing irregularly, in fact he was very relaxed, aware and happy. I asked him if I could make him comfortable, and he asked me to shake up his pillows so that he could sit up to say his goodbyes. I beckoned in his wife and two daughters and went to leave them for their final minutes together, but he held my hand and asked me to remain. He then held up both arms and looked round, gave us all a smile and said,' I am going home.' I immediately felt his spirit depart. We four ladies just looked at each other and all said together, 'What a wonderful death'.

The third patient's death was much sadder. The District Nursing Sister in the area asked me if I could meet her early the next morning, at a patient's house, to help put her on to an air bed to prevent pressure sores. This was a 50-year-old lady who had been bedridden for several weeks. She also had cancer, and had been in considerable pain requiring large and frequent doses of an analgesic mixture.

I met the other sister outside the patient's house, only to be told that she had died. She was extremely concerned by the circumstances. She had notified the GP, who had just departed having certified the death, the cause being advanced cancer. I was asked for my opinion and together we entered the house to view and lay out the body.

The patient's husband was very withdrawn, and we left him in the garden pacing up and down. We went into the bedroom and found a very cold and stiff body. Her husband said he had gone to London the previous day, and he admitted that he had told her before leaving 'You know what to do'. In his absence she had drank the full bottle of analgesic, as well as a full bottle of Paracetamol tablets which had been left on her bedside table.

There was a dreadful cold feeling in the room and the physical body appeared in torment. The spirit was still there, and I have no doubts that it was reluctant to depart so abruptly, before the allotted time.

This probably seems very fanciful, but I cannot find the words to describe my experiences with these deaths. It was as if I was being shown that the spirit can leave the body with varying time delays.

It seemed appropriate not to pursue investigations about the whys and wherefores of that death. It was obvious what had occurred, and one could only feel deep sorrow for the patient and her spouse's agony. It was fortunate that in those days political correctness had not taken over from compassion and common sense.

Through my nursing career I have witnessed many deaths. I have seen people die in agony, fighting the inevitable right up to the end; I have seen a slow but graceful exit accepted with bravery. I have realised with time that those people who have a deep religious faith are usually relaxed and ready to leave. They often prefer to slip away when the nearest and dearest have left the room, if only for a few seconds. Perhaps they are trying to make it easier for those left behind by avoiding a long-drawn-out farewell, or maybe it is because the patient does not want to be held back.

The grief process, for the loved ones left behind, differed from one person to another. The stages of grief were as diverse as the people themselves. I met the stiff upper lips who were unable to cry and those who wailed and tormented themselves with guilt for not doing or saying what they perhaps might have done with hindsight. There were also those who laughed uncontrollably, much to the horror of others in the family, a reaction which they could not prevent. I have spoken to other retired nurses who like myself have witnessed bereavement on many occasions from the tender teenage years. The common feelings we share are that none of us fears death or dying and we view a body as the empty shell which no longer provides a safe haven for the soul.

In addition to terminal care, the most frequent treatment I carried out was the care of leg ulcers. These are horrendous and extremely difficult to heal. I visited a female patient in her mid forties in a village near Kings Lynn when her nurse was on holiday. This patient had long-term ulcers on both lower legs. As soon as I entered the house I could smell putrefying flesh. The patient was lying on the sofa with extensive padding on both legs and sitting on the bandages were huge bluebottles. The sound of humming and the sight was like something out of a Hitchcock film.

When I took down the dressings I was relieved to see very clean wounds with no sloughing. This was because they were covered in maggots which were happily munching all the filth away, leaving very clean ulcers! That was my chance to write a paper for The Lancet. It wasn't until some years later that an Oxford orthopaedic professor wrote about this, when he set up a maggot farm to sell the produce to the medical profession to use on dirty wounds.

I liked and respected many 'old fashioned' remedies and found that honey was an excellent healer, and was often successful where antibiotics had failed. If I had my youth back again, I would study homeopathic remedies.

One case I visited was especially distressing. An elderly lady in the Fens lived alone, apart from nearly 30 cats to keep her company. Arriving at the small cottage it was easy to guess that the interior would be unsavoury. The exterior of the building and the garden were neglected. There were cats on each inside window sill, all looking as if they longed to escape, with their noses pressed against the glass. I had been warned to put piles of newspapers in my car together with plastic bags, and to make her the last case on my daily round.

On entering through the back door I threw papers in front of me so that my shoes, enclosed in plastic bags, did not touch the floor. I found the patient huddled in a chair next to a range which was unlit. I managed to persuade four of the cats sitting on her lap to abandon their mistress so that I could take off her filthy, ragged top to look at the wound below. She had untreated breast cancer, which had eaten away the skin and was protruding through the flesh. It was the most advanced case I had seen and there was very little to do to make her more comfortable, apart from applying a soothing dressing.

This lady needed to be in a hospice with 24-hour care, so she could spend the rest of her days in comfort. This suggestion was adamantly rejected, as she refused to consider leaving her cats. The whole of the floor was covered in excrement. The cats were never allowed outside and cat litter was nonexistent. The only food in the cottage was tinned cat food. My only option was to notify Social Services in the hope that with the RSPCA they could resolve the problem, but undoubtedly not to this persons' satisfaction. I could imagine how delighted the cats would be to get fresh air and a change of scenery.

My extended round when another nurse was on holiday or a day off meant I had to venture into remote Fen villages. The roads would run very straight until they suddenly came to a right-angled bend, which was very disconcerting, especially when the droves were shrouded in mist and the road suddenly curved around the deep drains. It was not unusual to see a vehicle upside down in one, especially if the road was icy.

Fortunately for me (though not for the victim), an accident had always happened long before I arrived on the scene, so I did not have to administer first aid. It cured me of putting my foot down, although I had often a long list of patients to find hidden away across fields of rich black earth.

It was not unusual to have to leave my car at the roadside and walk right across a field to reach the inhabitant of a farm cottage. On returning to the car I frequently found a sack of potatoes, cabbages, other vegetables or eggs left beside it, probably by a kind farmer who I never saw and certainly did not know, but who obviously knew who I was. The distinctive uniform did not allow me to get away with anything! If they left more than I required I would redistribute the surplus to a patient who I thought would benefit.

A difficult case to resolve, but a very sad one, was a titled lady who was a distant relation to royalty. She lived in faded glory and was in need of admission for long-term care, but refused to leave her four King Charles spaniels. She was bedridden and lived alone, with a chronic medical condition, in a huge upstairs room, shared with the four dogs. They were all riddled with fleas. Their rations consisted of a loaf of bread, a packet of margarine and a jar of jam.

A bottle of milk was the only other addition to their diet, and this was for patients and dogs alike! A well-meaning neighbour dropped these items off twice per week and left them on the bedside table. I kept hoping she would produce a shepherd's pie or similar, but suspect she had an ulterior motive for visiting this helpless old lady. I was worried she was suffering from malnutrition and ended up making an extra dish for her whenever I cooked for my own family.

She pronounced that she could not understand why housekeepers did not remain in her employment, 'It should be easy enough to discourage the rats in the kitchen' she said. Her imposing mansion was resplendent with priceless Chinese porcelain, as well as many valuable items of solid silver tableware, statuettes, antique tapestries, carpets and furnishings. Her son held a prominent national position. When I pointed out to him on the phone that not only was she vulnerable but the house was at risk, he simply said 'Oh, it's all insured'. I could have walked out with a fortune and no one would have been the wiser. What it is to have integrity!

The only safeguard I had was to invite the local constabulary to visit her and endorse my own concerns. After each visit I left her with only her beloved pets and cobwebs for company, finally flea-free, so at least no more itching, but with hopefully happy memories of a past life of splendour.

Until the final flea met its demise, I had to leave her until I had seen all my other patients so that they would not share the invasion. Every day I had to submerge myself in a hot bath, wash my hair and change my uniform.

A few weeks after I left district nursing to start work in a general hospital, this wealthy lady was admitted to a medical ward, alone to the end, with no pets, no cobwebs and no friends or caring family either. I know which I would prefer when it comes to my final saga.

There was also an octogenarian who was bedridden and had lived with her daughter and son-in-law for several months. I visited her for the first time at the request of her regular nurse who had a day off. I entered the house to find an unpleasant atmosphere. When I talked to the patient I discovered that there was no medical reason for her to stay in bed, nor did she have a mobility problem. Her daughter had confined her to her room - in fact she had been 'tidied away'. I suggested that I should help her to get dressed and sit in an armchair near to the window. I thought looking at the garden would ease her depression.

On taking off her night clothes I was horrified to find her upper arms and back were black, the bruises obviously identifiable as finger marks. She had been beaten on numerous occasions. This frail old lady was terrified. She had accepted that to be cared for by her daughter she should no longer have any expectations of better treatment.

It seemed the daughter was under pressure from her husband to get rid of her mother. She was tired and her loyalties were divided. I explained that the situation had to be rectified, that abuse could not be tolerated and that I would refer the family to a social worker who could assess the needs of the three people involved.

Why in these sad cases were the victims always females? How do men avoid ending up in such circumstances? Are they better at self-preservation, or are women really just living too long?

Not that men always look after themselves. There was one elderly chap who lived in a converted railway carriage, and one morning he got stuck in the seat of his outside toilet. The newspaper man flagged down my car to tell me he could hear him yelling for help. It was fortunate that he saw me, having himself ignored the cry for help

After managing to squeeze through the privy door (I was slim then, I would not be able to do it now!), I found he had slipped down into the bowl, having fallen asleep. His legs were in the air, his trousers were round his ankles and he looked very blue in the face. I heaved him up, cleaned his backside, which had a very deep red ring round it, and helped him into his carriage home.

By then we both needed a cup of tea. Just putting on the kettle was not an easy task. I had to fill a bucket of water from the well, light a primus stove, wash two enamel mugs, find a tin of Carnation milk and keep my fingers crossed that I would shortly be able to start my daily round of cases.

Another bizarre event came when I visited a patient to change a wound dressing. I was presented with thousands of £1 notes in biscuit tins, carrier bags, socks and in boots under a bed by an elderly couple who had realised just in time that the notes were going out of circulation. Did Sister know what they could do with this money, they wanted to know? I hastily drove them to the local bank, saw the manager and asked him to sort out an account.

This old couple's neighbour approached me, or rather waylaid me, one day, and demanded that I tell Social Services to put the couple away! I asked her why, as they were not a danger to themselves or anyone else. Her answer implied that it was because they were not socially acceptable. I wonder what that person is like now that she too has passed her sell-by date.

Another female I had to sort out was continuously using her toilet in the bathroom without flushing it. When the pan was full she then used the bath. Her GP asked me to visit. He said, 'Just pop in and see how she is, it is not a nursing problem, but just go and see what you think is wrong. I can't get to the bottom of it'. He would soon have found out if he had gone into the bathroom - or maybe he already had, I had my suspicions.

Nobody ever knew how I spent two hours of that day. It took a lot of rubber gloves, a plastic apron, a clothes peg and some ingenuity to resolve the problem. I will leave the details to the imagination. De-bunging a lavatory or emptying a bath of something other than water was not a nursing duty, but I could not walk away and leave it for the appropriate person - whoever that might have been

While nursing a patient in one of the local villages, I had established that there was strong evidence of witchcraft being practised. This was confirmed by the Church of England minister. He was so uneasy about it that before retiring to bed each night he would walk through the village sprinkling holy water. He said two previous ministers had left the village, having experienced satanic influences.

There was a picture of a witch on a village sign not many miles away, so perhaps the area had a history which I have yet to read about. I have to stop myself imagining that I was cursed when I deserted my district post for pastures new, as within two months, trauma struck my own family on a regular basis and continues to this day. When it became village gossip that I was leaving to work in the hospital, several people said I would come to regret giving up the care of the village folk.

I had been 'on the district' for two years when it became mandatory that we should all have a qualification in addition to our general training. To obtain this we had to attend college in Norwich for six months. This qualification necessitated us attending lectures, being observed while working with patients and being supervised by a qualified district nursing sister, a nursing manager and the lecturer. Then at the end of the day we had to write up case histories and submit assignments.

It was during this time that I met a male patient who had suffered from tuberculosis of a hip joint as a small boy, thirty years before. It was interesting to see that despite a pronounced shortening of the affected limb he had a good quality of life, and it reassured me that perhaps the youngsters I had nursed during my orthopaedic training, when I first left school, had perhaps also had a reasonable adult life.

I enjoyed being in the classroom with colleagues from all over the county. I was one of the newest district nurses on the course, as many of the others had been in post for more than twenty years. Some of them were very resentful, considering themselves experienced enough already and having no need for further training. I suspect they were actually rather outdated in their techniques.

The training strengthened our beliefs that our skills should be used appropriately, and supported us when we discouraged the misconception that we were supposed to do blanket baths. We were encouraged to concentrate purely on those duties for which only a registered nurse was trained.

There were several doctors who had to be re-educated about allocating what they considered were our duties. It was very satisfying to see them accept eventually that we were professionals in our own right. One woman GP had requested that I visit my own next-door neighbour, who had sustained a slight back injury and had been prescribed a few days' bed rest. The patient had wanted me to give him a bed bath and was taken aback when I suggested that his wife was fit and able, and if she could wash herself, she could also wash her spouse. Perhaps I would have acquiesced had he been a young, athletic hunk, but he was overweight and aggressive. I had seriously ill people to visit, patients who needed a professionally-trained nurse to administer to their needs.

I was not popular with that GP, who thought her word was a command which I should not question, and I had to ignore her snide remarks whenever I went into the surgery, especially when I also stopped my auxiliary bathing the mother of a retired doctor. The auxiliary nurse was only part-time and there were many elderly infirm living on their own who needed her assistance with their hygiene. I considered that the above lady could be helped by her very active daughter-in-law and that being a retired doctor did not give you the right to a handmaiden.

Allocating bathing needs was a juggling act, and to satisfy all the patients who really needed help with either a bath or a top and tail I should really have had two full-time care assistants. They never had time to accompany me when two pairs of hands would have been more comfortable for the patient and for my back. Instead of allowing this particular doctor to think that I was either idle or awkward, I should have challenged her perception of my role. The trouble was that I was just too busy. There were never enough hours in each day to retain nursing standards and give the care which I considered necessary.

During my final two years on the district, I encouraged patients to die at home rather than face hospital admission. Few hospices existed then. I was a great admirer of Dame Cecily Saunders and her philosophy that you should 'die living, not live dying'. The numerous terminal cases kept me on my toes, but looking after a person who is facing the inevitable end of their life is a rewarding privilege.

Their families also needed support, time and understanding. The biggest challenge was to help them all to be open with each other, to share the knowledge of the condition and prepare themselves for letting go. On the rare occasion when either the patient or the relative was in denial, there appeared to be a game of make-believe, with people not facing up to what was about to happen. Once the ice had been broken and I had built up relationships so that they would trust me, I would explain to the individuals why I considered that it would be easier if they shared their thoughts, fears and feelings.

Afterwards they accepted that the relief of not pretending helped the patient as well as themselves to come to terms with saying farewell. These cases always took time and could not be hurried. I had to learn to tread a fine line and not to become emotionally entangled, becoming so drained I had nothing left for my own family.

Five years after working in the community I was given the opportunity to attend a one-week course at Bristol Cancer Help Centre, not as a patient but as the supporter to a close friend who had secondary cancer in her liver.

In this very caring establishment I was given an insight into enhancing quality of life for cancer sufferers. It confirmed my own feelings that they need a sympathetic environment in which the patients and their partners can feel safe to share their feelings and fears about a life-threatening illness.

Each morning at the centre began with reflection in the chapel, led by a minister or member of staff. No specific denomination dominated or intruded and attendance was optional. It appeared to set the tone for the day and introduced a spiritual dimension, perhaps helping to ease the burden within some hearts, opening minds to new approaches or maybe to reintroduce the Holy Spirit into life through increased awareness.

Programmes of therapies were tailored to each individual's needs. They included visualisation, meditation, reflexology, therapeutic touch and counselling. I especially enjoyed the massage therapy. The blend of massage and herbal medication eased many tensions and the foot massage was welcomed and indulged in by all the course members

The days passed very quickly, as the course was intensive and everyone, including the supporters, experienced fatigue due to the emotional demands. The message from the staff was to direct your own destiny and do not let others decide how to fill your needs. The week was full of 'gifts' generously shared and given to enable an emotional energising and healing within oneself. It was a rediscovering of childhood, of feeling loved, protected and valued.

I learned to receive and to be given care, and in developing an increased self-awareness I felt free to be my own self and to let go of the clutter in my life and the situations which intruded into my inner peace of mind.

With the new insight into holistic care, I wished that I had been better informed during terminal care nursing in the community. I now knew how the patient with pain, fatigue or depression can be comforted with a foot massage and how the bereaved, injured and 'burnt out' can benefit from counselling. I learned how staff and patients can be refreshed with relaxation classes and support groups, which can ease stress and restore harmony. Peace and tranquillity in our homes and hospitals would facilitate an improved quality of care, and be more conducive to the healing of the whole body, mind and spirit.

During my fourth year driving around the villages as a 'ministering angel', I was asked to go on another course at the Suffolk College in Ipswich. This was so that I could become a practical work tutor, in other words a senior sister who would train qualified general nurses new to community nursing before they took their exams for a district nurse qualification. It meant back to the classroom, lectures to attend and dissertations to be handed in. I wondered why in middle age I was subjecting myself to the extra stress of trying to prove to others what I could do in my sleep, or indeed standing on my head.

The tutors both had health visitor backgrounds, but their hands-on experience had stopped many years previously when they had assumed teaching roles, which I felt made their opinions less valid. One day I was so fed up of listening to yet another boring lecture that I took an extended lunch break, meeting up with a friend and missing the early afternoon lecture, to the tutors' dismay. Up to then I had received an A for every essay, but that day I got only a B. It was about terminal care, a subject close to my heart and one I had no trouble writing reams about. But this insulted man nitpicked over it and used his red pen whenever possible.

I qualified as a tutor but never managed to put the qualification to use. This was because, while I was still attending college, I saw an advertisement in the nursing press for a new post, and immediately set my heart on it. It was the position of Liaison Nursing Officer, based in the West Suffolk Hospital. This was an opportunity to rectify the appalling discharge procedure which was still being implemented during my time district nursing, not only by the local Health Authorities but nationwide. Patients were discharged to their homes, even after surgical operations, with no follow-up care. The local milkman and paper delivery man were often the first to know the patient needed after-care and would flag down my car. They would notify me that there were sutures to be removed, dressings to be changed or injections to be administered – in fact they had all the information which had not been given to the GP or myself. This was an intolerable situation, and I could not wait to put matters right.

I was delighted when my application and subsequent interview were successful. This was the beginning of the most rewarding years of my nursing career, even though they were not spent at the patients' bedside. That is another story, of the days when I wore yet another hat, faced yet more challenges and had to re-educate more people. The staff reported to me, referring to me as their 'intrepid leader'. I wonder why?

1978 - 1982
West Norfolk Health Authority - District Nursing Sister

The Church of Our Lady and St Stephen - Lynford, Norfolk

1982 - 1991
West Suffolk Health
Authority - Nursing
Manager

Chapter Nine

LIAISON NURSING

My new post proved a great contrast to the life I had known. Thirty years after embarking on a nursing career, in 1982 I found myself with a role which did not involve hands-on nursing, but which did require all my communication skills.

The previous health-visitor-trained Nursing Liaison Officer had been performing the task, ensuring that the community health visitors were kept informed of paediatric admissions but with little communication with other community staff about general patients. This explained why I had received so little information when 'on the district', and why the local milkman knew more about the nursing requirements of recently-discharged patients than anyone else.

The interview was held in the West Suffolk Health Authority main offices in Bury St Edmunds and was conducted by the Chief Nursing Officer, Mr Denis Gobel, and his deputy, Mrs Mary McLaren. It comprised in-depth questioning by both of the interviewers, so I was fortunate in having identified what was missing in the current provision. I did not hesitate to tell them that under my jurisdiction it would be administered quite differently.

I wanted to start with a completely clean slate, a real new broom with new policies and procedures, all of which I outlined. They were immediately compliant, and agreed that it was time to close the hospital-community gap and think about the transfer of patients from one environment to the other, instead of their admission and discharge.

So I put on yet another nursing uniform. A visit to the hospital sewing room introduced me to a very helpful seamstress who showed me the very attractive navy blue fabric, which she would make up to my own design. This took me right back to the Far East, where I had sketched dresses in pencil on scraps of paper for Indian or Chinese tailors to run up clothes overnight.

I chose a short-sleeved mandarin-collared dress with a zip up the back and matching long-sleeved jacket. The sleeves and collar were edged in white piping and the belt had a silver buckle - my 'security blanket'.

This exalted position also required me to have a part-time clerical assistant, and my interviewing experience came in very useful when recruiting applicants for this position. For the majority of my ten years in post I had an excellent extra pair of hands and I could not have managed without Kath Harris, who acted as my personal assistant. Her efficiency, clerical skills, common sense and loyalty enabled me to run the department on oiled wheels.

Before I could start providing a liaison service, I had to devise an acceptable carbonized form in triplicate on which the nursing staff could convey information to the appropriate community carer. Nothing is straightforward in the NHS. Everything has to be approved in a committee which will haggle over the most inconsequential details, using delaying tactics to avoid spending money.

To prevent crisis intervention following a transfer, there needed to be a better understanding between all personnel. Relationships could only be established and roles understood and identified if the various disciplines communicated with each other and shared information.

The delivery of care is often multi-professional and with multi-agency involvement, so it had to be based on mutual understanding, trust, respect and cooperation. I believed that the barriers between hospital and community might then disappear and the continuing needs of the patient could be met by staff communicating with each on a regular basis, breaking down barriers and working as a complete entity and not in two different camps but as components of the same National Health Service.

Like Martin Luther King, I had a dream, but there were a few nightmares before it came to fruition.

It took me four years to establish an effective communication link between voluntary and statutory personnel who provided care on a district-wide basis. Systems were implemented to collect, collate and distribute information, and relationships were established by the recognition of other people's roles. This ensured continuity of care where it was appropriate for all geriatric, paediatric and general acute and medical patients when they transferred from hospital to home.

I had to re-educate the consultants and make them appreciate that they could no longer tell a patient on their ward rounds that they could go home that day. They could only say that the patient was medically fit for discharge. Other aspects of patients' needs had to be identified, firstly making sure that the right provision of care was in place.

The consultants soon appreciated the multi-disciplinary approach to patient care and were grateful for the advice and assistance given by those professionals with an interest in the patient's well being. My suggestion of weekly ward meetings was accepted, so that where severe problems with a patient's continued care were identified a case conference could be held to bring every aspect of the situation out into the open, utilising not only input from the hospital services but also from those in the community.

One case conference was held to plan a package of care for a married couple who were both patients. The main concerns arose because the elderly husband was adamant that they should be discharged home together, yet he was a bilateral amputee and his wife was very confused. Neighbours, friends, GP, home help and nurses all voiced their concerns about the situation. The main carers were invited to the case conference, where the husband 'took over' the chair which I normally occupied. Within an hour a very successful meeting was concluded to everyone's satisfaction and a package of care was formulated. It allowed this devoted couple to spend their last few years together in their own home without further intervention or readmission to hospital. Importantly, it also allowed them to continue to be responsible for regaining and retaining their own independence.

Every day I worked in this department was different. No two patients ever had the same needs. One might have needed his toenails cutting every six weeks, while another needed someone to walk her dog daily. They all required a separate assessment, each a balanced and objective viewpoint. Once more my experience in a personnel department was useful.

As the liaison service grew in credibility in the acute and paediatric areas, it needed to expand so that it covered all the departments and wards in the district general hospital and the two smaller hospitals in the group. This was needed seven days a week, as patients were also admitted and discharged on Saturdays and Sundays.

I applied for extra funding so that I could recruit nursing staff to assist me, the main essential qualification being that they were either district nursing or health visitor trained. Like myself they would be based in the general hospital but have community experience and understanding. I wanted them to resist becoming institutionalized in the hospital environment. The ability to remain objective was essential, so that pressure was not exercised by misplaced loyalties. I did not want them to promote one view or another, but to retain a balanced approach. To achieve this I wanted funding to come jointly from both the hospital and the community budget.

The liaison nurses had to be creative and imaginative thinkers with analytical and interpersonal relationship skills. They had to be qualified to undertake and reach informed decisions on the information which was collected. Only then could patients be transferred and continue to receive the necessary care to avoid readmission.

There was tremendous job satisfaction in ensuring not only that patients received any continuing care they needed but in promoting a better understanding between hospital and community and helping them to work as a team.

In 1986 I introduced a new policy to the health authority; the discharge procedure now stated that all patients referred to a district nurse would have a follow-up visit within 24 hours of discharge. With the increased emphasis on community care, especially in the present climate, I consider this has become even more essential. It is common sense that the majority of elderly people prefer to stay in their own homes, cherishing their independence as long as possible. It is also desirable that expensive acute beds should not be 'blocked'. It is however, morally unacceptable if speedy discharge does not lead to genuine aftercare.

The needs will vary according to people's physical, mental and social conditions, so a flexible approach is vital. When the patient is first discharged the needs are greater and the support more urgently required. Elderly patients confuse the issue by making unrealistic estimates of their ability to cope. In the protective environment of the hospital they can all too easily imagine that they will be able to manage at home. Friends and neighbours promising to fill the gap can be a highly unpredictable source of help. More community resources are obviously necessary in the face of the growing numbers of elderly, not less.

As the service I had started gained credibility and spread regionally and nationally, I began a local liaison nurses' forum and then a forum for the Royal College of Nursing. Meetings were held quarterly both locally and in London and representatives came from other health authorities. Gradually continuity of care was recognised as an essential service, and my discharge procedures were implemented nationwide.

In 1989, as the Manager responsible for Nurse Specialists for the West Suffolk Health Authority, I received an invitation to speak at the Royal Society of Health on 'Continuity of Patients' Care' and was given in appreciation an inscribed crystal goblet. In years to come, if it remains unbroken, it may provide a talking point on the Antiques Road Show. I wrote many articles for several nursing journals, and it gave me a wonderful platform to proclaim the gospel according to Jan and the bee I had in my bonnet about patients' aftercare, all because my ego had been dented when the milkman had known about my patients' needs before I did.

I am once more getting on my soap box. As the years creep up on me I become increasingly frustrated by the failure of our once-excellent NHS to provide basic care. The complex technology of modern medicine is all very well, but if the basics are missing what is the point of extending life? Surely quality of life is more important than quantity.

When I retired in 1991, I felt that in all the aspects of nursing care in which I had ventured, I had fulfilled my role to the best of my ability. That was more than 20 years ago. In the future I wonder how many retiring nurses who have trained under Project 2000, the nurse training introduced in the late 1980s, will be able to make the same declaration with conviction? The worst change was to take student nurses in training from patients' bedsides and put them in college to learn basic patient care from tutors, most of whom had never nursed .Once these newly-qualified nurses are on the wards they retreat behind paperwork to avoid spending time at the bedside. I ask myself if this is because they do not have the confidence, as they do not have the basic nursing skills and are out of their depth in the presence of the patients. The

United Kingdom had the best Registered Nurse training in the world. It was not broken, yet it was 'mended' just the same by those who would not listen to what the 'old timers' had to say.

Matron did know best!

Chapter Ten

RETIREMENT IS NOT FOR THE FAINT-HEARTED

I welcomed retirement, thinking that my nursing days were behind me and there would be no more hats to be worn, as I could not see myself wearing a mob cap or hairnet. It was at last time for my husband and me to spend more time together. We enjoyed walking, especially in the Yorkshire Dales and planned to travel frequently up the A1 to indulge in this hobby.

But within six weeks of enjoying waking up naturally instead of with an alarm clock, fate intervened and my first two years of intended luxury came to an abrupt end. Once again I had to put my nursing skills to good use, but this time it was closer to home. Sarah one of our daughters had to have two brain tumours removed, and being fiercely independent had returned to work as a nanny in London. Then our youngest daughter Kate sustained multiple fractures in a road traffic accident on a motorway near Liverpool.

We received a telephone call from the Accident and Emergency Department of Broad Green Hospital notifying us that Kate was seriously injured and was about to be taken to the operating theatre for major surgery. It took a lot of persuasion to get them to give me

1991

Spinal injuries unit - Southport

My very own patient, Kate

At last, retirement. No more hats!

the details of her injuries. The thought of driving five hours not knowing what to expect was horrendous.

That long drive was the beginning of five months of driving back and forth to be with our daughter during her hospitalisation, initially in intensive care and then in the spinal injuries unit to which she was transferred. The unit was understaffed by nurses, so once again my sleeves were rolled up and the care of Kate became a priority. I was adamant that the surgeon would not surgically intervene when he wanted to operate on her fractured spine. Mother's instinct convinced me that she would regain some sensation and movement in her lower limbs which were paralysed.

Without an operation she would have to be nursed lying flat for twelve weeks, as opposed to being up in a wheelchair within two weeks of surgery. This would obviously demand more nursing care, but I was prepared to undertake this to maximise her opportunity of regaining improved mobility. My previous experience in orthopaedics and surgery was invaluable.

I contacted a doctor friend I had met in Hong Kong thirty years before to ask his advice about my daughter's additional fracture of her femur in her left thigh. In my estimation sufficient interest was not being taken in this injury, and I wondered if it was considered unimportant as she would not walk again. However the recovery of her broken arm was essential so that she would be able to self-propel a wheelchair.

It was all worth it when I received an early morning call from the physiotherapist to say that some movement had returned to Kate's toes. Denis and I were staying in a bed and breakfast place five minute's walk from the hospital. It was the beginning of a remarkable partial recovery. Instead of spending her life in a wheelchair, some periods are now spent walking on elbow crutches. She can lead a full and active life, having returned to full-time work within a year of the accident. She is also married and living in the Middle East, where she is trying to instil awareness of wheelchair access difficulties in public places.

With this sort of difficulty being faced by a nearest and dearest, I have become acutely aware of how ignorant so many people are when faced with a person who is physically challenged. The saying which illustrates this most clearly is, 'Does she take sugar?' and how refreshing it is to see some enlightened people when they unselfconsciously sit or bend down so that they are at the same level as the wheelchair user. It cannot be easy for anyone with a mobility problem when their faces are always in line with other people's groins.

During these last twenty years varying experiences have given me tremendous understanding and awareness of the difficulties which are faced by anyone who has a physical impairment as they go about their daily life.

The most profound insight into poor mobility has been through my own deterioration. If I was young and fit again I would be an excellent nurse on a unit for care of the elderly.

I cannot really pinpoint when I reached my 'sell by date'; it may have been when we moved house for the third time after retirement, or perhaps been when my head hit the concrete after tripping on an uneven driveway when I was loading the car with flowers, intending to arrange them in the local village church. My arrangements of flowers never again graced the altar, or even a window sill. My flower arranging days came to an end when I found it was a dangerous balancing act climbing onto a pew to reach high window sills with a heavy vase in my arms.

To replace that hobby I needed a sedentary occupation which I could enjoy sitting in a chair, preferably a self-adjusting one which I could operate by pressing a button to raise my legs or assist me to stand upright.

Crocheting filled that gap for several months, with my fingers quickly learning how to use hooks of various sizes to slip a stitch and do double chains, treble chains and more complicated patterns to make flowers, which I sewed on to crocheted bags, hats, scarves and throws. My husband had a throw crocheted in his regimental colours of green, red and black, my daughter had one to cover a sofa and there are two more which still have not found homes. Eventually my wrists and fingers began to ache so much that my hobby was carefully put away, hopefully to be resurrected if a cure for arthritis is discovered. It may have occurred because I am addicted to cheese and chocolate, both of which I have read can be a cause of these very painful joints.

My next hobby was to acquire a laptop, which I mostly use as a word processor, but of course it had a magnetic attraction and enticed me on to the internet, where I could explore all the retail stores which I could not explore in the flesh because of my limited mobility. My passion for clothes was aroused, as it was so easy to press a few keys, think up a password and await the arrival of the post or courier with yet another outfit. Initially these were chosen for outdoor wear, until several months passed by and they remained in the wardrobe, unused and still enclosed in the plastic covers in which they had first arrived. Now I order more practical trousers and pullovers, chosen for comfort to be worn around our home.

It is marvellous, however, to be able to order my weekly groceries on the internet and have them delivered to the bungalow door. I wonder if I can get the delivery driver to put it away in the freezer and larder if I learn to look even more pathetic.

I also found Google Earth and now frequently venture forth to rediscover all the places where I have lived, visited or worked. I do wish that the new occupants of the cottage we owned in Wensleydale had kept the doors white and not painted them blue, and I wonder how they managed to get building planning permission for an extension.

I did confuse an equally elderly friend who was a neighbour at our previous address, when she telephoned and I commented on the change of door colour. She thought I had driven past her house without calling to say hello.

Then I decided to write about my eventful life. The most difficult part of that decision was how much detail to include and how much should I leave out. If and when it was completed, should it be finished with a hard back or a paperback? I wondered if it would solve the puzzle of what to give for Christmas presents to my five offspring and nine grandchildren.

It would be interesting to hear their comments when they know about my misspent youth. Perhaps it would also be a reminder that I too had an active life once upon a time, especially if the book contained photographs of me in and out of uniform. It is a pity that I never had a photograph taken wearing a bikini, which might prove that I did not always have a spare tyre.

Every Saturday I attempt to complete the Times crossword. If I cannot find the answers to at least half the clues, I will know that it is not only my body that is deteriorating. Until then I need not face that problem, provided I can still see to read my Fact Finder book when I am looking for the answers to composers, planets, mythology and other non-essential information which my brain does not retain. By erasing irrelevant facts and figures, I hope my grey cells will remain healthy and be sufficient for everyday essentials.

I have decided to try and keep warm so that hypothermia is kept at bay. I know it can cause confusion, and I am desperate to continue to be aware of the day and time, as I do not want the window cleaner to find me in bed at 11 am. Other decisions to be made are whether I should turn up the thermostat to seventy degrees (not centigrade, I hastily add), or would it be better to find some thermals on the web? And if I wear cashmere socks, do I have to wash them by hand, which my nobbly knuckles would not like? I wonder if I can find some red flannel bloomers, and perhaps a woolly nightcap would compensate for the loss of hair on the top of my head - I did not think to crochet one. I am grateful for the winter fuel allowance and the free television licence. A small compensation if I do acquire short-term memory loss will be that I can watch all the repeats and not remember seeing them previously.

I put my feet up after lunch to prevent my ankle from swelling, which also gives me an excuse to nod off for a few minutes. Then I can stay awake long enough to watch University Challenge on the TV at eight pm. I always hope that someone will be present to hear me when I know at least seven of the answers - that is, if I have first understood the questions.

Listening to music is a pleasure, but singing for me is becoming a disappointment. When I try to join in the hymns when Songs of Praise is shown on a Sunday evening, all I can hear is this thin reedy voice which is unable to reach the top note, which is annoying when I can still remember all the words. I must try being a contralto instead of a soprano. I wonder if Gareth Malone could help me to find the right pitch? After all I am an ex military wife. He could train another choir and help some ancient Brits to form a silver haired band.

Eating at midday is more beneficial for my hiatus hernia than later in the day, and with the exception of a small mug of warm milk at bedtime I avoid too much liquid in the evenings so that I do not have to get up in the early hours of the morning. The podiatrist keeps my toenails trimmed to prevent me from tripping over them, and the hairdresser visits to cut my hair short so that after washing it under the shower it dries quickly and I do not have to use a hairdryer, which makes my shoulders ache.

In my seventies I have put on weight and developed lumps and bumps in all the wrong places. I have to try and make my white curls cover bald patches, stiletto heels are now too precarious for my poor balance and I wear sensible one-and-a-half-inch heels. Elastic waist bands are more comfortable, and front fastening bras are easier for my arthritic finger joints.

I am trying not to think about why the ageing process can be unkind, but just accept and grow old gracefully. It is just a stage in one's life cycle which everyone reaches, some sooner than others. It is better to adjust and come to terms with the loss of mobility and the worrying about where the nearest lavatory is and learn how to compromise and not feel guilty about taking short cuts or leaving the films of dust which occasionally accumulate.

It is fortunate that the majority of 'oldies' can retain their long-term memories. I comfort myself with remembering the daily ward rounds in a general hospital taken at a brisk walk, attempting to make sausages on a factory production line; clamping artery forceps on during major surgery, watching fishing boats returning to harbour in the Far East; attending investitures at Buckingham Palace; passing-out parades at the Royal Military Academy Sandhurst; university degree ceremonies; excursions to exciting places and living in exotic countries. There are so many wonderful memories of all the different hats that I wore to keep me company during a night when sleep is evasive.

I must try not to feel negative about my shrinking height as my vertebrae collapse, my skin wrinkles and my arches fall. With determination I will continue to retain my independence even if it is with the aid of a perching stool, elbow crutches and a trolley on which to balance trays.

I miss the admiring glances from the opposite sex and being able to drive the car, which I much prefer to being a back seat driver navigating and nagging. It would be nice to have an audience to listen to my opinions about how to put the world to rights. I am saddened that a celebrity culture has crept into Great Britain and that many high-profile jobs are grossly overpaid. I wish there were more billionaires, or even millionaires, like Bill Gates who would use their wealth to help the less fortunate. It would be better also if so many people did not believe that they were entitled to so much without contributing to society. The 'want' word is so often voiced- I do not want to grow old but I do not believe it is my entitlement to remain young!

If I am not careful I will fall off my soap box, and then I will experience a taste of my own medicine.

Different Hats

1981   1983   1988

2009